I0473661

Inventing Success

5 Steps From Idea To Shelf

By

Jon Hoffman

Contents

Introduction

Let's be honest here. You didn't pick this up and start reading because you thought it would be a nice way to pass the time, or because you expected a heart warming story about a crippled girl and her pony. You are reading this for one reason—you have an idea for an 'invention' and you'd like to know how to turn that idea into a product that people will buy; and ultimately, you want to make a lot of money from it. And if you had even the slightest clue as to how to do that, this book would be hanging in mid-air, about to crash to the floor as you burst through the wall *Wile E. Coyote-style*, and disappeared over the horizon to put your plan into action. But you're still here aren't you?

*And I'll bet I know something
else about you…*

Every day, you see people who are not as smart as you making millions off of mediocre ideas while your brilliant inventions languish in the cob webbed corners of your basement. You can't figure out what the difference is between that rich, smarmy bastard hawking the latest cooking gadget on TV and you, flipping hamburger patties every time the buzzer goes off, while the blueprints for your time travel machine remain hidden in your sock drawer. You have no idea why one invention 'takes off' while most never see the light of day. It's infuriating.

You want a piece of that pie, don't you?

I'm sure that at this point you think I'm either a mind reader or a cloying jackass, but neither is true (except for the cloying jackass part)—I'm simply working the odds. The vast majority of people I have encountered are toting around an idea that they feel has some value; but they have no idea what to do with it. So you're not alone. But that doesn't help you, does it? Just because there are a bunch of people in the same boat doesn't mean they're sailing happily off into the sunset. Titanic, anyone?

So what you really need is the key to this whole affair—a key that is going to set you apart from the rest of those folks—you need the magic wand, or secret recipe, or ruby slippers, or whatever the hell it takes to turn you from a wannabe into a genuine, bona fide, successful inventor. And I am going to give you that…

But before we start, let's look at some of the reasons you're here.

Why you're not already an inventor

While it may seem like an impossible fantasy to get paid for an 'idea,' or it may appear daunting and intimidating to come up with something truly *new*, or to deal with the many details of designing or manufacturing a product, the simple truth is that the very progress of humanity depends on innovation and invention, and every single day ordinary people have ideas and come up with 'inventions' which have the potential to advance our culture by steps which may be monumental or may be infinitesimal-- but large or small, there is an enormous thirst for such innovation—an ever present opportunity—and there is no reason why the next 'big idea' can't be yours.

Actually, that's not entirely accurate. There are lots of reasons why that next big idea won't come from you. You're too busy, you don't have any training in that area, someone will probably just steal your idea anyway, you don't have the extra money to invest, you're not handy and couldn't possibly build a prototype—you can come up with a million reasons why it's not worth your time or effort to even try. And you'll do such a good job of convincing yourself of this that you won't feel the slightest twinge of regret about missing out on something that could have been really big. After all, haven't you just built an airtight case as to why there really *isn't* an opportunity?

You have identified the problem, you have looked at it from every angle; you have come up with incontrovertible retorts to every possible objection that could be raised. You have applied great thought and consideration to formulating the 'optimal' solution.

You diligently identified and pursued one course of action to arrive at the desired result—*the perfect excuse why you shouldn't bother trying to be an inventor.* Do you see the irony here? The very talent and effort that you have enlisted to create a compelling case against the possibility of success is precisely what is needed to bring an invention to market. If you had focused all of that energy and effort on developing your idea, you'd be a real inventor by now.

Here's one more depressing thought for you:

The difference between the guy sitting on his couch watching infomercials for other people's inventions and the guy sitting on his yacht enjoying the rewards of his own inventions is simply this—that second guy actually *did* something. He wasn't smarter or better connected or luckier—he just put one foot in front of the other and actually made the effort. And what is preventing you from being that guy on the yacht? A great big, insurmountable-- *nothing.* There is absolutely no reason you can't be that guy. All you have to do is try. Just do it.

Wait a minute—'just do it?' Does that somehow sound familiar? Sure, that's a slogan coined by Nike, an enormous corporation known for innovation and invention. Oh, that figures—that's where all inventions come from, right?—giant corporate monoliths with multi-million dollar secret laboratories filled with geniuses in white lab coats.

Think again. Nike is indeed a giant company-- a true world class innovator and international icon. But do you know where Nike came from? Did it just appear one day, an instant multi-billion dollar enterprise that sprang up overnight? Obviously not. It was the brain child of a guy named Phil Knight who started out with a little idea and an even smaller business. From selling sneakers out of the trunk of his car, he is now on the Forbes top ten list of the wealthiest Americans.

Does the name Bill Gates ring any bells? You may know him as the richest man in the world, but it would be better to think of him as a guy who had an idea (a computer operating system) which took him from tinkering in his garage to his current position of nearly unimaginable wealth, power, and history altering influence.

I could fill the next hundred pages with examples and case studies of regular people who turned an idea into an empire; or at the very least great wealth. But you don't need me to do that. Go spend an hour on the internet and Google the rags to riches success stories of the great inventors of our time (it might even be worth Googling Google) and you'll see for yourself. But there's something else you'll see—a pattern will begin to emerge as you study the big success stories—and it is this pattern that holds one of the keys to their, and your, success as an inventor. Every one of these individuals has one trait in common.

Perhaps counter-intuitively the great inventors, indeed the most successful people in industry, politics, religion, and pretty much every enterprise you can imagine are not all blessed with genius IQs, were not born to wealthy parents, did not all attend Ivy League universities, did not get 'lucky breaks,' or belong to secret societies. Some were quite average in their intelligence, some were born to families as poor as dirt, some dropped out of school quite young. There is only one trait shared by every single one of these successful people throughout history—*perseverance*. They just kept trying, and eventually they succeeded. Check out the story of Abraham Lincoln's life sometime. While he is remembered by history as one of the most successful, influential people ever, his record of failures is almost comically extensive. He went broke, had businesses fail—pretty much everything and anything that could go wrong did go wrong—in most cases two or three or four times; but honest Abe kept dusting himself off and eventually became the man whose great accomplishments we all know. And he didn't exactly have good looks to fall back on. If that ugly bastard can do it, so can you. Persevere and you will prosper.

And here's the best news of all. Perseverance is not a genetically determined trait. It's not one of those things that either you're born with or you're not. It's not something that some people can do and others can't. It's a decision. You look in the mirror and you say to yourself, "I'm going to keep trying. I may have failures, and it may be hard or discouraging, and it may just plain suck, but I'm going to keep going, even in the face of tremendous adversity." And that's it—like flipping a light switch you go from being a quitter to a person who perseveres. And succeeds.

But perseverance is just one of the pieces to the puzzle—you also need some specific knowledge-- the tools, the building blocks, the fundamental understanding of what inventions are, how they are conceived and refined, what makes them valuable, how they are protected, how they become products that people will buy, and perhaps most importantly, how they become money in your bank account. It's not like you couldn't figure it out for yourself-- I did, many people have. But it also took me the better part of twenty years of trying to really understand how the process works. I'm offering you a shortcut. Be smart and take it.

So let's review—you don't need me to give you the ideas—you already have those. You don't need me to tell you not to quit—you already have the iron will and perseverance you need to succeed. What you don't have, what you need, and what I can give you, is a road map for what to do and where to go with those ideas. In short, you need a primer on how to be a successful inventor. And that, my friend, is precisely what you will find on the pages that follow.

Wait a minute—why am I giving away all of my secrets? If I really do have some insights to share, if I really have the inside scoop on how this invention game works—why the hell would I share that with you? Doesn't that 'pull the rug out from under me?' Won't I somehow lose something valuable—the 'mystique' or exclusivity of what I can offer my clients? Doesn't this prove that I'm full of crap and I'm just trying to con you into buying a few worthless pointers that anybody could cobble together and pass off as being worthwhile?

In short— no. I could care less how many "inventors" are out there roaming the streets. I spend most of my time enjoying my life and having fun. I only work on projects which interest me. I'm not competing with anybody. I live my life and pursue my interests, and when I stumble across something that I think could be done better, or I start looking for something I want and find it doesn't exist, I'll figure out how I think it should be done and make a few phone calls to see if I can drum up some interest. Period. I don't sit on the internet or on the phone all day long calling up prospects saying, "I'm the world's greatest inventor—hire me;" or, "I'm the only inventor who really understands how this game works—I'm the one you need;" so it won't hurt or affect me one little bit if suddenly the world has a whole bunch more smart people out there who can legitimately call themselves inventors.

The bottom line is this—I'm not competing with you or anybody else. The world has a lot more room left for inventors. Not to sound too high minded or *goody-two-shoes* about it, but I'd be downright happy to have a few more people out there fighting the good fight and coming up with stuff I'd really like to have—a cell phone that actually works, a human interface for computers that's natural and intuitive (just talk to your computer instead of using a keyboard and mouse), hell—a flying car wouldn't suck. Get it? I've got nothing to lose, everything to gain— and come to think of it, so do you.

Be the Author of Your Own Success Story

You may have noticed a little *double entendre* (that's 'double meaning' for those Francophobes in the cheap seats) in the title to this book—you could just as easily interpret "Inventing Success" to mean either 'success at inventing' or 'creating (fabricating) success.' This was not unintentional--*because this book is very much about both*. This is certainly a primer to, or perhaps more accurately a road map through the rocky terrain of intellectual property development—but the bigger picture is that a mastery of the skills, techniques, and knowledge contained herein equips you in a very real sense to create something out of nothing—in the course of developing ideas and inventions, you will also be creating a livelihood, a lifestyle, an identity, and--- success.

I have broken down the inventing process into five discreet steps: Problem Solving, Proof of Concept, Protecting Your Idea, Refinement, and Monetization. By working methodically through each of the five steps you will have the best possible chance of successfully commercializing your invention. Of course, each step is different for every invention, but all of the same principles apply. This book is a detailed exploration of how to successfully complete each step with enough specific information to be useful, and enough general information to be sufficiently flexible to cover virtually any type of invention.

Be patient as you read this book-- we already know what you want-- the simple, straightforward answer to the question "how do I make money with my invention?" without having to wade through a bunch of froufrou crap to get it. And you will get this answer; but don't be impatient and jump ahead to the section about 'licensing your invention' because that's all you really care about—stick with me as I lead you through the whole story. The material may at times seem obvious or irrelevant, but I assure you there is a method to my madness. I have been 'inventing' or developing intellectual property for over twenty years with some success, and in that time I've refined my understanding of how this game works. The information I'm giving you is being parsed in a deliberate, logical, well-conceived way. Each step leads to the next and relies upon the preceding. Inventing is a process which involves many pieces, all of them equally important, so 'skipping ahead' doesn't get you to the 'good stuff' any faster—it just causes you to miss a few of the vital building blocks which are crucial to solid foundational understanding. Read it all, digest it, absorb the 'big picture' and then move forward with your own invention.

That's it-- it's very simple. Start working on your invention today. Put one foot in front of the other and keep at it. If you fail, try again. If you get knocked down, get up. If you stick with it, you will ultimately succeed. That's what the history books tell us. But that's also what I'm telling you. I am a successful inventor. I have come up with many, many ideas. Some of them were lousy. A lot of them were good. A few of them were great. I tried to sell all of them. Most were rejected. But I kept at it and ended up making a lot of money from my inventions. Not overnight. Not the first time. But over the years, by sticking with it, I have become a successful inventor—and you can become one too. As history has clearly demonstrated, and as I have seen in my own life, if you keep trying, ultimately you will succeed.

Okay, enough with the pep talk-- now it's time to sit

down, shut up, start reading, and let the information soak into your brain. This is going to change your life.

Overview

It would be easy to argue that inventing is an incredibly complicated, nebulous experience which is impossible to break down into discrete steps given that every invention is by definition new and therefore has no precedent. But that is not entirely accurate. Of course every invention is new (or it wouldn't be an invention), but the 'process' of invention is relatively simple, straightforward, and predictable. No matter how complex, esoteric or revolutionary your invention, you will still go through the same basic steps as you develop your invention from that initial spark of genius to a product on a store's shelf. An understanding of these steps makes the invention process far more accessible and less intimidating, and also acts as a yardstick to indicate how far along you are and what challenges remain. I have broken the process down into five steps as follows:

- Problem Solving
- Proof of Concept
- Protecting Your Idea
- Refinement
- Monetization

Here is an overview of what each step involves

1. Problem Solving. **Sometimes referred to as 'creative ideation,' the very first step of the inventing process is coming up with the idea. I prefer to call this step 'problem solving' because the best inventions are not simply new ideas, they are solutions to problems which already exist. In this section we will talk about what makes an invention, where ideas come from, the phenomenon of concurrent invention, and more.**

2. Proof of Concept. **In the technical parlance of inventing, this step is called 'reduction to practice,' but both terms mean the same thing: taking an idea which exists only in your brain or as a sketch on a napkin and turning it into a tangible, real-world object which performs the desired function. This step is sometimes referred to as 'bread-boarding' because it isn't about making a polished, shiny, prototype— it's usually a crude, unattractive mish-mosh of parts which don't look anything like the finished product, but which demonstrate that the idea can be made**

and will work. A very important part of the Proof of Concept phase is that this is when reality and the laws of physics will refine and improve your idea into something viable.

3. Protecting Your Idea. Once you have reduced your idea to practice and figured out the nitty gritty of how it can actually be produced, it is time to protect the idea so others can't steal it. This is where we talk about patents—one of the most misunderstood areas of inventing.

4. Refinement. An idea is not a product. The idea first has to travel the long road to demonstrable prototype with the security of some form of protection; and that prototype ultimately needs to be refined into something which is producible, economical, functional, robust, and aesthetic before you have something you can call a product. The refinement phase includes industrial design, engineering, consideration of manufacturing materials and methods, understanding fixed and variable costs, branding,

packaging, and more.

5. Monetization. Here is where the rubber meets the road—selling your invention. There are two basic routes you can take: licensing, or manufacturing and marketing. We will discuss the advantages and drawbacks of both. No matter how tempting it may be to jump ahead to this chapter, remember that all of the value is established by following the first four steps.

By presenting the information in the order I have, I'm laying the foundation of concepts that you need to understand in order to grasp each successive step, and eventually stand confidently on your own two feet as a knowledgeable, credible, successful inventor. Each piece is important in its own right; and while you may not see the connections right away, hopefully everything will fall into place and paint a cohesive, compelling picture by the time you get through it all. There are no shortcuts or magic formulas— it takes plenty of hard work and perseverance to successfully bring an invention to market. The scary part is when you don't know what to do and have no road map to follow. This book will give you the path; but it's up to you to put one foot in front of the other and take the journey. It won't always be fun or easy, but it will give you the best possible chance of succeeding as an inventor. So get ready for some hard work-- like Edison said, "Invention is one percent inspiration, ninety nine percent perspiration."

Step One: Problem Solving

What exactly is an invention?

Let's start at the beginning and define our terms. After all, if we're about to go dashing off to refine, develop, manufacture and market our inventions, we had better be in agreement as to what exactly an invention is. Let's look at a few examples and see if we can suss out a definition.

Would it be fair to say that my latest notion-- a diesel powered hover toilet that can transport me to work at the speed of light while I'm taking a crap-- qualifies as an invention? Not quite—it's very likely a *new* idea, but it takes more than that to make the cut. In order for something to be an invention, it has to be not only a new idea, but one which is *practical*, or can be reduced to practice (made into an actual thing that works). So until one of those thousands of new inventors I'm spawning knocks on my door with a prototype, my flying crapper resides squarely in the realm of fantasy (or dementia).

My next idea, which I'm quite sure can be made, is a gold plated cheese grater with built-in harmonica, mounted on a gyroscopically stabilized unicycle. That's gotta be an invention, right? Indeed, by the standards above it qualifies as in invention—it is novel (new) and it can be reduced to practice (made)-- but there is a further distinction that needs to be explored—the *value* of an invention. By value, I don't mean the monetary value or market value (although these are closely related), but rather the utility or usefulness of an invention. Does this invention serve a purpose or address a need? The need doesn't have to be utilitarian (making electricity or chopping onions)—it can be completely frivolous—it makes people laugh or gag or dance. Unfortunately, one would be hard pressed to find a need, let alone a *tolerance* for my one wheeled musical curd shredder, so it doesn't make the cut as an invention with utility either.

How about a self-canceling turn signal for motorcycles? Let's see—it's practical (this is an actual invention of mine and I have a functioning prototype); it's novel (there have been other attempts to do this, but they don't work, mine does); and it has utility (this addresses an existing, non-trivial need in the marketplace). So, yes, this would be an example of a legitimate invention.

We now have a definition of an invention which reads something like, "a practical, novel idea which has utility." And that's pretty much it—every invention can be measured and defined by the degree to which it satisfies or expands the boundaries of novelty (how distinct is it from related ideas?), utility (does it serve a purpose that someone recognizes as having value?), and practicality (the ability to be made). We'll talk about each of these factors in much greater detail later.

What exactly does an inventor do?

But first, let's talk a little more about what it means to 'invent' something. It is rare indeed that an idea is truly 'new.' While my hover toilet above would seem to be a pretty new concept, in reality it is nothing more than a number of existing, well known ideas thrown together in a 'new' (albeit absurd) way. We are all familiar with toilets, diesel power, things that hover and things that go really fast. Of course, the technical details of how one makes a diesel powered toilet hover, or how one makes anything travel at the speed of light were just plain fudged—I haven't figured out how to do that (and Einstein would have a few things to say about the possibility of anyone ever making something travel at the speed of light). So let's look at something a little more realistic.

My self-canceling motorcycle turn signal is truly a novel invention. It solves a known problem in a technically viable way which can and has been reduced to practice, and it does it in a novel way which has not been done before. But is it truly 'revolutionary' in the sense that it employs fundamentally new ideas? Not at all. Basically, I have combined what I call 'state of the shelf' technologies (technologies or technical solutions which are currently in use) from disparate fields, and made them work together in ways they haven't been asked to before to perform a new function. So is it novel? Yes. Is it an invention? Absolutely. Does it represent a major new idea or category of thought, or is it radical or revolutionary? Not even a little bit. But it does illustrate a point— most 'inventions' are clever, novel re-applications of mechanisms, processes, materials, technologies, or functionalities which are already well known in another field. It may involve making something smaller or lighter or using it in a way which wasn't originally intended or conceived, but it is very likely a re-positioning or refinement of something already known.

Know a little about a lot

This 're-positioning' is not a bad thing. It is a tool for you to use and exploit to your advantage. It is something to be aware of and embrace in your journey as an inventor, and in your quest for ideas, solutions, and inventions. And it should underscore the desirability, advantage, and even necessity of knowing as much as possible about as many things as possible. Soaking in all of the information you can about how things work, how things are made, what new developments are happening in every field of endeavor from mathematics to aerospace to ice cream making will expand your 'tool chest' or pool of creative resources and give you a wider, more powerful selection of 'tools' to bring to bear on the problems which come before you in your career as an inventor. And even if you don't know about lots of *different* things, but have some expertise in one *particular* area, see if you can't reapply that knowledge in a far removed field.

This raises another important point: as our world grows increasingly complex, and as the sheer volume of information grows exponentially, it is inevitable that people working in any one field of endeavor will become narrowly specialized. It simply is no longer possible to be successful in a given field and be a generalist. People in a particular industry are usually so focused on the specifics of their industry and have allocated such a large percentage of their energy and resources to their struggle to assimilate a body of knowledge which is growing at an accelerating rate, that they cannot possibly devote any of their time to following, let alone studying the particulars of the immense range of new developments and achievements in all other areas of endeavor.

While somewhat daunting, this means that opportunities abound for someone who can solidify their position as a generalist. Someone who maintains a long view—who studiously preserves their view of the forest while taking cursory notice of the specifics of the individual trees, is ideally positioned to do what we've just determined is done with most 'inventions'—to perceive opportunities to apply known solutions in one field to seemingly insoluble problems in another. To this end, I make it my business to know what's going on in the world; but I don't do this for mercenary reasons-- I do it because I'm naturally curious. I like to understand how things work; I like to see how problems have been solved.

In fact, when people ask me what I do for a living, I generally do not say, "I am an inventor." I usually describe myself in a different way, which I feel is more accurate. I say, "I am a dilettante."—or someone who dabbles in many fields and knows a little bit about a widely divergent range of topics.

Where do ideas come from?

Even though you already have your million dollar idea, it may be worth taking a moment to think about where ideas come from and how one cultivates them, for several reasons—first, if you plan on making a go of it as an inventor, you will find that you need a lot more than just one idea, and second, you should understand the concept of concurrent independent invention (two or more people inventing the same thing, or having the same idea at about the same time without copying, influencing, or even being aware of one another) which happens more often than one would suspect.

Look at it this way—we all live in the world together. Very few people live in caves, literal or figurative, to the extent that they are not aware of what is going on around them. And with mass communication being what it is—the internet, satellite TV, radio, etc., we not only have an unprecedented awareness of what's going on all over the planet-- there's a massive homogenization taking place globally. It used to be that you could travel to a far away country and see things you never knew existed-- experience cultures, traditions, foods, ways of life that were completely alien from your own. But as the world becomes smaller by virtue of communications technology, pretty much everyone knows what everybody else is doing and how they're living, and what their lives look like; and everybody has snatched up the best bits to call their own. Now, you would be hard pressed to go anywhere on the planet and not find a McDonalds, or people talking on cell phones or people dressed pretty much the same way, living their lives in what has become a frighteningly uniform way, all the while drinking a Diet Coke.

Concurrent invention

And as much as you like to think of yourself as a free thinker, an independent spirit not caught up in or tied down by the conventions and mores of our bourgeois world—you and everybody else on this planet are entirely, inextricably, unambiguously a product of our cultural context, or environment. And since *your* environment is increasingly similar to everybody else's environment, and since our thoughts, ideas, needs and inspirations are in large part determined by our communal environment—it shouldn't come as a surprise to learn that the brilliant idea you just came up with may, in fact, have just dawned on one or two or a thousand other free thinking, independent souls just like you.

How can this be? Strange as it may seem, almost all ideas are derivative in nature—they are evolutionary rather than revolutionary. What do I mean by this? Simply that new things tend to happen in little baby steps—small incremental improvements over existing things which cumulatively, over time, will produce major changes. It means that ideas come from *somewhere*—they don't simply materialize out of the blue. It's just like Darwin's theory of evolution where he posits that random mutation, or arbitrary variations will be tested by the environment and only those variations which give their host some advantage will be passed on and become a surviving, continuing trait of the organism. If enough of these adaptations occur, you have an entirely new species—or a very big change relative to where we started. Darwin did not postulate that *entirely new animals* suddenly appeared and were tested by the environment—it was very subtle variations of *existing* animals that were the subject of his work. The difference between Darwin's theory and mine is that nature creates random, arbitrary changes whereas I'm operating on the assumption that our erstwhile inventors are consciously making the effort to introduce changes which will improve or benefit the original concept. Some will work, some won't; but the point is, they all derive from what already exists, what is already known. And why is this? Why don't we operate from a clean slate, start with virginal fresh ideas untainted by the world we live in?

This is in large part the result of our minds and lives being so intimately steeped in the concrete realities of what already exists that we can't truly liberate ourselves from an awareness of these things, and every thought or idea being tethered to the world we know. Not that this is a bad thing. Most people just blindly accept what exists and never stop to challenge or contemplate how this could be changed or improved. It's only a small group of individuals who veer from the sheepish masses and dare to think 'what if?' or 'why not?' And much more often than not, these bold questions are less about a completely new, radical proposition, than a modestly novel improvement to the status quo. It may be a clever improvement, it may even be brilliant, but it is very likely an 'incremental' improvement to something which already exists rather than being something truly new. And in most cases, the improvement itself is not new but instead a clever application of something that exists in a different form in a different area of endeavor which has been transplanted to its new home and dubbed an 'invention.'

Perhaps surprisingly, in most cases the germs of these new ideas are not themselves new, but innocent bystanders in the relentless march of technological progress which get snatched up by savvy, observant 'inventors.' And this is how a number of people come up with the same idea at the same time, quite independently.

Here's an example. Let's say everybody has a widget in their home and all widgets work pretty well, but they're just too damn heavy. Then some hardy adventurer, in his explorations of the last undiscovered frontier, stumbles across a vast grove of strange trees, the wood from which has the peculiar characteristic of being ultra strong and lightweight; but our intrepid explorer has no idea what to do with this stuff. All he can manage is to bring home a little sample which promptly gets stowed in his closet, and he then gives the strange trees a cursory mention in a little article he writes for the barely circulated monthly newsletter published by his local chapter of the explorers' club. As it happens, a handful of the subscribers to this journal also happen to be widget owners, and one or two of them have just used, or are indeed in the process of using their widget as they read this little blurb about these curious trees. The first raises his eyebrows, then grabs another handful of Doritos and goes back to watching the game on TV. The other puts two and two together, and voila—we're well on our way to a new, lightweight widget-- an 'invention.'

Here's a somewhat more concrete example of the evolutionary and cooperative or parallel nature of innovation: it would seem that one of the most revolutionary, totally new inventions in modern history was the airplane. What could be more radically new or different than people suddenly taking to the skies to travel when previously they had been limited to relatively primitive earth-bound conveyances? Well, if it had happened that way, you'd be absolutely right. If people were trotting about in their horse drawn carriages and stumbled upon a Boeing 747, it would indeed by a shocking, radical, utterly new invention—a revolutionary rather than evolutionary change in the world. But that's not how it happened. It happened slowly, methodically, in baby steps—some of the baby steps were brilliant and crucial, but they were still small incremental steps in the overall gradual evolutionary process. Man had long yearned to escape his earthly binds, and the first hint that this might be possible was seen as far back as 400 B.C. when the Chinese began experimenting with kites. Over the years, the aerodynamics, materials, and engineering of kites matured and they evolved into unmanned gliders; and eventually a number of people got the idea to make these gliders big enough to carry a human being aloft. The first experimental outings were dangerous and unstable, but gradual improvements in the understanding of aerodynamics and the commensurate improvements in stability and control made glider flight relatively safe. But it wasn't until an unrelated invention—the *internal combustion engine* came onto the scene that people began to contemplate powered flight. The heretofore ubiquitous steam engines were too bulky, so when the gasoline internal combustion engine burst onto the scene, the potential for powered human flight took a big step forward. It wasn't the Wright Brothers alone, but rather a small number of Americans and Europeans who more or less concurrently realized that a lightweight internal combustion engine made powered flight possible; and they all pursued it more or less independently. There were a number of powered flight attempts prior to the Wright Brothers' historic December 3, 1903 flight, and there is some debate as to whether the Wright Brothers deserve to be credited as the pioneers they are widely regarded to be; but this is hardly the forum to debate this detail of history-- I bring it up only to illustrate the point that their 'invention' of powered flight did not occur in a vacuum, nor were they the only ones pursuing it.

Ultimately, it was unrelated developments in materials science, electronics, navigation, and a hundred other fields, all of which eventually found their way into the design of aircraft, which gave the modern airplane its form and function.

This should convey a number of points—sometimes more than one person will have the same idea at the same time; sometimes developments in other fields make possible huge advances in totally unrelated areas; and sometimes the credit, the glory, and the money for an invention can be unfairly, disproportionately, or even arbitrarily accorded to only one of a number of potentially equally deserving 'inventors.'

So the notion of ideas or inventions springing from the knowledge and experience base that most of us have in common, as well as the importance of the confluence of other developments and technologies in making 'inventions' possible or practical should serve both as a lesson and a warning: pay attention, we are surrounded by fertile ground, but the operative term here is 'we'—you are not the only one aware of these opportunities.

As an interesting side note, it's worth mentioning that this process is not necessarily smooth and continuous. It sometimes falls into a lull, and then shoots ahead in an instant. And oftentimes the catalyst for the next 'burst' of invention is a news event, perhaps well publicized, perhaps not. It could be that a scientist somewhere catches a fish that propels itself through the water not by wagging its tail back and forth, but by sending a series of pulses—sequential circumferential expansions and contractions down the length of its body. This makes a great page 17 blurb in the bigger metropolitan newspapers, and makes big splashes in the esoteric journals read by marine biologists-- overall, not much of a blip on the radar in terms of global news and information dissemination. But you happen to see it and it gets you thinking—what if I adapted this biological means of propulsion through water into a mechanical means? Would the military be interested in it for a new form of silent undetectable underwater propulsion for submarines or in a scaled down version, for hand held pods that could pull a Navy SEAL through the water? Would commercial or even pleasure boat manufacturers be interested in some variation of the same thing? How about toys? Is there something cool, or novel, or promotable, or better yet—really inexpensive to manufacture about this that would suit it particularly well to an application in the toy business? Wait a minute—could this be adapted to another kind of fluid dynamics—air? Would it be possible to introduce an entirely new class of pro-pulsion devices for air travel? The possibilities here are endless, and this one news blurb could be the catalyst for a world changing invention for you—or the other five hundred people who read, and took note of it.

Is it still possible to come up with a new idea?

Should you even bother then? If so many people are exposed to the same raw information every day, and some percentage of them is likely to have the same insights or epiphanies as you, why waste your time trying to develop your invention when it is likely that a bunch of others will be engaged in the identical pursuit?

The answer, which is to me in equal parts depressing and encouraging, is that you should absolutely do it because your greatest ally is human nature—most people are lazy and reactive rather than ambitious and pro-active. A lot of people may have the same idea at the same time, but very few will act on it. And of those few who do, fewer still will have the knowledge, tools, or resources to exploit it commercially.

Market driven inventions

There are two basic types of inventions: the kind that are clever, novel gadgets that you have to explain to people and convince them why they need one, and the kind that solve an existing problem in the marketplace. It is much easier to sell the latter variety. Here's an example of what I mean. Let's say you invent a lawnmower that not only cuts your grass, but can plant tulip bulbs as it rolls along. It's a pretty cool idea, but I've yet to run across a middle aged, slightly balding and pudgy suburban homeowner sitting on the curb in front of his house, head down on his arms folded across his knees, sobbing inconsolably because he isn't able to plant tulips while he cuts his front lawn. It's just not a problem that weighs heavily on the minds of many people. If, however, you sat down on the curb next to this poor soul and eloquently explained to him over the course of the next few hours all of the tremendous advantages of being able to plant tulips while cutting the grass, you may very well convert him to being a loyal customer for your new gadget. And if you could walk up and down the well manicured streets of residential neighborhoods all across the country, you could very well persuade a veritable army of vaguely discontented suburbanites that your invention is just the ticket to lift them from their malaise. But that's a lot of walking, and even more talking. Of course you could do a similar job with lots and lots of commercials on TV, or ads in magazines and newspapers, but that gets expensive. The point here is that an enormous effort is required both to make people aware of your invention and to convince them that they want or need it.

If, however, you invent something that people the world over are already clamoring for—a cell phone that actually works, for example—the hordes will literally beat a path to your door. And by implication, it will be much easier to communicate the merits and commercial potential of your invention to, and secure a licensing deal from, a manufacturer—if they clearly see why people will want to buy your invention, they will clearly see the monetary value it has.

The point is this—it is an easier sell if your invention solves a problem that consumers already know they have, as opposed to affording them some benefit or advantage that they have to be made aware of or educated about. And that is what I mean by 'market driven inventions.'

Some people dismiss 'improvements' to existing products as being less creative, valuable, or worthwhile than truly new 'inventions.' This is nonsense. We've just spent a fair amount of time talking about how every invention is both contextual and evolutionary. An improvement is simply that—an evolutionary enhancement to an existing idea.

Not only is there no shame in improving something which already exists, it can be a much faster and easier 'sell' than an invention with no ready reference or point of comparison. The very progress of civilization depends on such improvements and many an inventor has made a comfortable living doing nothing else.

Another great potential benefit of an 'improvement' invention is that you can create a proprietary advantage in a commodity marketplace—if you come up with a unique feature or benefit with strong perceived value, you can become the 'must have' product in a crowded field of similar items and sell for a much higher price and make much more profit.

The sole caveat here is the recognition that sometimes the product which you improve is itself proprietary and you can't manufacture, market, or sell your improved version without permission from the original. In such cases, you have only one potential market for your invention—licensing to the original product manufacturer; and this could dramatically limit your opportunities for success. So a word to the wise—when your invention is an 'improvement,' try to make an improvement to a public domain or commodity product where you have free reign to sell a better version without infringing anyone's patents or stepping on any toes. More about this in Step 3.

No idea is precious

What?! This is heresy! How can I possibly suggest that your million dollar idea shouldn't be coddled, nurtured, groomed and protected with your very life? Well, for a number of reasons. First, as we touched on earlier, the idea is the easy part. Even a brilliant idea may just not be practical to make into a product and successfully commercialize. Second, you may not be the best judge of how good an idea really is. I know I'm not. I don't really consider myself to be 'average' or an 'everyman;' and since the most successful products are those that appeal to the masses, to the lowest common denominator, I not only suspect, I am quite sure and proud of the fact that I have little in common with my buying public. Third, as we've already discussed, the odds of success for each invention you come up with are appallingly low. If you realistically hope to be successful, then play the odds and come up with a whole bunch of ideas/inventions so you improve your chances that at least one of them will 'hit.' And finally, sometimes an invention just isn't going to work out. As we mentioned before, there are plenty of examples throughout history of great ideas that never went anywhere because they were ahead of their time, or because of poor business decisions, fate, bad luck, or whatever.

So sometimes you have to recognize that it is time to move on. We spoke earlier of the importance of perseverance, and I would never suggest for a moment that you shouldn't try and try and try some more. But at some point a reasonable, rational person must say, 'enough is enough' and move on to the next project. It's one thing to stick with it and try every possible angle to coax success out of an invention, it's another matter entirely to fail to recognize when it's time to bail out, and instead ride it flaming into the ground.

I'm not telling you to abandon your inventions after the first rejection letter. I'm telling you to hold on to them loosely, nurture them and allow them to evolve in view of feedback you get and information you will inevitably garner in your attempts to market them or find a licensee. Don't be so married to your ideas that you smother them or they crush you—allow them to evolve organically—even transform completely as circumstances warrant. And if it ultimately becomes clear that it just ain't gonna happen for this one—let it go. Move on.

The simple facts are these: some of your ideas may be stolen, even the really, really good ones; some of your ideas, even those you have the highest hopes for and invest lots of time, money, and energy in refining and developing, will turn out to have been already thought of by someone else; and some of your ideas, in fact most of them, will very likely just be flops and go nowhere.

I have always said that anybody who is really concerned about any one of their ideas being lost, stolen, or abandoned is in the wrong business. The invention game is not for anyone whose ideas are so precious. Ideas are like grains of sand. If you are trying to build a mountain out of sand, you have to keep pouring lots and lots of it onto the pile, and most will just slip right back down to the base. But eventually, the base grows wider and the mountain rises. And even though the grains of the sand that slip down to the bottom don't seem to be doing anything, don't seem to be important at all—each and every one serves a purpose. Even the grains at the bottom of the pile which contribute nothing to its height have to be there to support the ones higher up. And like those grains of sand, every idea, even the ones that don't go anywhere, contribute to your knowledge, experience, and confidence as an inventor.

So be prepared to come up with lots of ideas. It's a numbers game. The odds of success are very low, but the laws of probability state that even with a very low probability of a particular outcome, as you increase the number of trials (attempts) the overall likelihood of realizing the desired outcome will commensurately increase. In other words—throw a lot of spaghetti at the wall and eventually one strand will stick.

Outside the box

You've probably heard the term 'thinking outside the box.' It's reasonably self-evident what this means— coming up with ideas and solutions which are un- conventional. But I'm hoping that the term 'box,' which is a bit of a throwaway, now takes on new significance in light of our discussion about the con- straints upon and commonalities amongst all of our thinking. 'Thinking outside the box' isn't just some glib saying referring generally to a more creative way of looking at a problem— it is a direct, specific indictment of the very real boundaries which con- strain our thoughts and ideas, imposed on us by our social conventions and shared experiences.

But once you become aware of the degree to which your thinking has been confined by 'the box,' you should find it much easier to venture beyond these limitations. Understanding and recognizing that a boundary exists is the first step in moving beyond it.

Every time you come up with a new idea, ask yourself

where it came from, what the influences were-- why that idea? And every time you dismiss an idea as impractical, unrealistic, or impossible, ask yourself why you have imposed such judgments. You may be surprised to learn that a great deal of the value we attribute to ideas is quite independent of their intrinsic worth, and more closely aligned with the tacit system of values with which we are imprinted.

Know what you're talking about

It is surprising how often I'm approached by people who have a 'great' idea which is illogical, insane, or defies the laws of physics or gravity or known science. There's nothing wrong with wanting to develop something which hasn't been done before, but at least make an effort to understand the field you are proposing to revolutionize. For example, I have been contacted by several (unrelated) people, each of whom had the 'brilliant' idea of putting generator/ motors on 2 or more wheels of a car in order both to propel it and harvest power by converting kinetic energy to electrical energy when braking. All of them seemed to feel that this would create a vehicle which would never need gas or recharging, because all of the power would come from the wheel-resident generators. Great idea—except for those pesky laws of physics and things like conversion inefficiencies which screw the whole thing up.

At the end of the day, this concept is sort of like lifting yourself off the ground by pulling on your own hair. It's fine if you don't know the history of the global quest for the perpetual motion machine. It's fine if you don't know what kinetic energy is. But we live in a world today where virtually anything you could ever want or need to know is only a mouse click away. So click the mouse. A lot. Educate yourself about the field in which you choose to work. Being an idiot isn't just embarrassing; it's a waste of time.

The point is this—be intellectually curious, be creatively extravagant—free yourself from the shackles of conventional thought—but make the effort to familiarize yourself with enough basic science or logic or history to recognize when your ideas have slipped from the realm of inspirational to the void of insanity or illogic.

There are no bad ideas

It is easy, and oftentimes tempting to knock an idea or characterize it as stupid, or lame, or hopeless. For example, my hover toilet idea is pretty clearly and unambiguously a 'crackpot scheme.' But it would be a mistake to criticize it. Why? Because in our quest for answers, solutions, and ultimately 'inventions,' the greatest obstacle we need to overcome is our reliance on, and adherence to the status quo, the mundane, the 'rules' as we understand them about how things work, what is possible, what is 'good,' and what could actually be 'real'—or reduced to practice. Sometimes, the 'wackier' an idea is, the more it liberates us from the shackles of conventional thinking. For example, the hover toilet is a pretty 'out there' notion, but implicit in its conceptualization are a couple of properties and features which are anything but wacky, and which may lead to real, novel inventions. What could possibly have value in this mad scheme? Well, perhaps the idea that a toilet doesn't have to be stationary, and might be incorporated into a means of conveyance isn't entirely new (there are toilets on buses and airplanes) but it does raise the question as to why we shouldn't re-think not only a toilet in our personal, daily mode of conveyance, but lots of other things as well—who says that our house needs to be anchored to the ground, fixed in one location—or our shower or breakfast table? In other words, the cockamamie notion of a hover toilet, at its core holds a legitimate germ of an idea, or at the very least a springboard from which we can begin to contemplate an entirely new line of thought—a new perspective on a very static area of inquiry. We have always just assumed that toilets, showers, etc. belong in the house and can't, won't and shouldn't move. But what if they did? How could that change our lives, make them better, more efficient?

This points to the value of the 'blue sky' approach to searching for 'answers' to problems which may be specific (e.g. you have been charged with coming up with a better way of doing 'X') or may be general and undirected (e.g. you are basically day-dreaming, trying to come up with any old invention at all). Attempting to remove limits, constraints, and most importantly, negativity from your thought process can be a surprisingly powerful tool for 'supercharging' your imagination and creativity. Sometimes 'absurd' equates to 'fertile' in the creative ideation process. Remember—there are no 'bad' ideas—every thought, every hare-brained scheme has implicit value, even if it is only to highlight avenues of inquiry which need not be pursued.

There are, of course, limits to this. The 'blue sky' approach is a wonderful tool to be used at the beginning of the idea generation process, but it should probably be put away by the time you get to the production engineering phase. If you're sitting at a production review meeting with a bunch of engi-neers and, in response to a question which comes up about how they should perform a functionality test while the production line is moving, you propose that a team of nymphs hover over the conveyer belt and sprinkle fairy dust on the components-- at this point you are no longer a daring and brilliant 'free thinker'—you are a frigging idiot.

There is a time and a place for unfettered 'free thinking;' but this will never forgive ignorance, or serve as a substitute for a solid understanding of those very concepts we are trying to shed (tempo-rarily): how things work, how things are made, the laws of physics, what consumers want, need, and care about, how much things cost, etc. Like so many things in life, it comes down to 'balance'—know when to let go of these things, know when to cling tightly to them.

One more thing to think about with respect to 'bad ideas'—many inventions have actually risen from the ashes of failures, or hypotheses that didn't pan out. A very famous and very lucrative example of this is 'Post-it Notes.' These ubiquitous yellow sticky pads were not the object of a carefully conceived and targeted development program. They were instead the entirely accidental result of an unrelated experiment gone wrong. Somewhere in the labs of 3M, a researcher was trying to come up with a special kind of adhesive for a new product. He came up with a formulation that didn't work—it was a low-tack, non-aggressive adhesive that didn't stick very well and then just pulled right off—leaving no damage or residue. Not at all what he was trying to come up with. But lo and behold, someone's quick thinking, open mind, and marketing savvy turned this dud into a huge invention that actually defined an entirely new product category. Moral of the story—keep your mind open to the possibility of finding inspiration and success in the most unexpected places—even your own failures.

The beauty of being wrong

In our competitive society, we have come to dread making mistakes. Our culture seems to equate being wrong about something as tantamount to being a failure as a human being. But this is one convention we must quickly shed if we are to be successful in the invention game. While many think that inventors must have huge egos to support them in crises of self-doubt, quite the opposite is true. Ego can be the enemy of creativity. If you are overly concerned with what people will think of you, particularly if you make a mistake, you have imposed yet another constraint on your ability to 'break through' the already formidable cultural constraints on free thinking.

Think about this—if you are to invent something truly new, truly novel—then by definition it has never been conceived before. If no one has ever had this thought before, there is no pre-existing understanding as to how it should be envisioned, what is good or bad about it, what is right or wrong. If it is a new thought, it is yours to define. This is not to say that you can't get it all wrong—but even in getting it all wrong, you will very likely have opened the door to a new understanding, a new perspective, a new way of thinking about a problem—and since this new understanding is a significant piece of the definition of an invention, you will at this point be one very large step closer to a proprietary solution.

Of course, all of this 'free thinking' must ultimately be tempered by a solid understanding and acceptance of the realistic constraints of physics, logic, market realities, etc.; but it is easy to see how liberating it can be to rise above, if only for a time, the shackles of what is 'practical' during the creative ideation phase of intellectual property development. This ability to free oneself from the debilitating fear of being wrong is a crucial part of the 'blue sky' phase of the invention process.

One of the biggest and most common mistakes I see people making is falling in love with their invention. They come up with an idea and suddenly it becomes the entire focus of their existence. They eat, sleep, dream, and think of nothing else. So what's the problem? Isn't this simply the perseverance I've been yammering about?

Unfortunately, no. Passionately pursuing an idea is wonderful and vital. Wearing blinders and being able to see only your particular embodiment of an invention is dangerous. Why? Because you may not have gotten it right the first time. You may have missed something. There may be an entirely different way of solving the same problem. There could be a solution which is cheaper or stronger or more attractive or more environmentally friendly. And if any of these is true—not only is your invention not going to be as good, or cheap, or attractive, or robust, or environmentally friendly, or super groovy as it could be—you may have just opened up a great big window of opportunity for a potential competitor. Here's why—if you come up with a brilliant invention, and then spend the time, money, and energy to get it out into the marketplace, and you have the good fortune to create a lot of consumer awareness and demand—there will suddenly be a whole bunch of people who are now aware of this new opportunity and you better believe they will be trying to find a way of cashing in on this lucrative new business you've created.

So how can they do this? Easy—did you miss something? Could they simply add a new feature, or change the color or use a better material to make their version of the product more desirable? Could someone figure out how to make the same product less expensive without compromising quality or durability? Is there a way to make your invention more fun, more attractive, cooler, or more environmentally friendly? Any of these could completely derail your future success; but there's an even greater danger. What if there's a completely different way of solving the same problem? What if you created market demand for a solution, but you didn't figure out the best of several possible ways of addressing that need?

I've seen this happen many times. Someone identifies an opportunity in the marketplace and comes up with a really smart invention to address that need. But then they fall in love with their invention and completely lose sight of the big picture—and miss the fact that there may be other fundamentally different solutions to the same problem. In short, there are generally many ways to skin a cat, and if you fail to consider all of them and insure that you are going to market with the very best one, you are simply handing the opportunity to an inventor whose mind is more open than yours.

How can you avoid this pitfall? Easy—focus on the opportunity, not your solution. Once you have come up with your invention, put it aside and attempt to solve the same problem a completely different way—or maybe the same way but from a different angle. Consider how a competitor might try to knock off your product, or capitalize on the opportunity which you have created. If you focus on the opportunity rather than the solution, you have a much better chance of creating a valuable and defensible position in the marketplace.

Step Two: Proof of Concept

The idea is the easy part

Thomas Edison is famously quoted as saying that invention is "one percent inspiration and ninety nine percent perspiration." He meant that the idea is one thing, but reducing it to practice, doing all the hard work to actually make it viable is where the men are separated from the boys. Perhaps if we look at an example which illustrates the magnitude of effort involved in developing just one of his many inventions, it will help elucidate what he meant by this.

Edison came up with the nifty idea that passing an electric current through a piece of wire would make the wire glow, producing light—the basis for the incandescent light bulb which illuminates our world. Simple, right? Absolutely. The problem is that just passing an electric current through any old piece of wire, in the presence of air, will pretty much vaporize the wire instantly. It took Edison years and literally thousands of experiments to hit upon the idea that his concept would only work if the filament was protected by a non-reactive environment (in a vacuum or inert gas filled glass bulb), and then thousands more to work out the precise metallurgical composition of the filaments that performed best once the reactive environment had been removed. Ninety nine percent perspiration indeed.

There is a crucial and rather frightening fact to bear in mind here—by definition, when you are 'inventing' something—everything you do has never been done before. You are truly out on the tightrope with no net. It's not like you're following a set of blueprints or a recipe and you know exactly how things will work out when you're done—you are blazing a new trail and there are no guarantees that the trail will lead anywhere. It may be a dead end, it may be filled with poisonous snakes, or it may drop off a sheer cliff—you just keep bushwhacking, making as much progress as you can—sometimes veering this way or that, sometimes backtracking to follow a more promising detour you had earlier shunned. Successful inventing is about 'trying'—it is about an empirical implementation of the 'scientific method' wherein you develop a hypothesis, conduct an experiment to test that hypothesis, then based on the results of this experiment either modify your hypothesis or change one variable in your experiment and try again. And again and again. Sometimes things fall into place; sometimes they fall apart. Then you start over. And this is how—painstakingly, methodically-- an 'invention' is slowly dragged out of the treacherous waters of 'ideas.'

The breadboard

An idea is just an idea until it has been reduced to practice—rendered tangible and demonstrable. There are all sorts of ways of doing this, but the most rudimentary and practical is what's known as a 'breadboard.' A breadboard is a model or physical interpretation not of the invention in its totality, but simply of the critical or novel aspect of the invention. What I mean by this is the breadboard is used to prove out the viability of the core essence of the invention. Unlike a prototype which usually both looks like and works like the final product (but very likely has been handmade at enormous expense rather than having been produced with the intended manufacturing methods), a 'breadboard' is usually a clunky, awkward, Rube Goldberg-esque contraption that exploits any means available to demonstrate concept. The actual term 'breadboard' refers to a specific type of electronic circuit board designed for quick prototyping which permits wires and components to be 'plugged in' without having to be soldered. This 'plug in' system makes it quick and easy to build, modify, and test circuits, as well as to reuse the hardware for another project. It also results in a pretty crazy looking 'rat's nest' of wires and components which certainly don't resemble a product visually, but should be able to reproduce functionality accurately. So the breadboard is basically a quick, easy, sometimes messy way of proving that your idea can actually work.

Here's an example: when I was developing my electronic message display wheel system which was eventually marketed as PimpStar wheels, I first needed a breadboard or proof of concept model to communicate to a potential licensee what I was talking about and to prove that I could really do what I said I could do. So I worked with my electronics engineer to build a very clunky looking model which had a big electric motor mounted on a stand, which spun a large round circuit board that had some LEDs mounted on it. When the circuit board spun around, the LEDs lit up and displayed a message. This breadboard looked nothing like the final product, didn't use any production components, wasn't built using any of the ultimate manufacturing methods, and didn't include any number of design elements or technical solutions which ultimately became part of the final product. But it did clearly demonstrate that I could produce a stable image using LEDs which were rotating on something round (which could be argued to resemble an automotive wheel), and it wasn't too much of a stretch to see how we could get power, and communication signals, and speed and position sensing apparatus into the wheel as well.

And it worked—it was a good enough demonstration that answered enough of the tough questions and left only those easier questions (the answers to which could be easily grasped), that I was able to sell the invention based on the breadboard alone. Of course there were several years of intensive development to solve all of the functionality, real world durability, cost and aesthetic issues that distinguish a 'product' from an 'invention;' but it was a very good first step.

It can't be done until you prove that it can be done

The point is this: an idea means almost nothing until you can prove that it works. An idea for a teleportation machine is a joke—a functioning prototype of a teleportation machine is the greatest invention ever, worth unimaginable sums. But this is an extreme example. Most ideas are smaller and less radical than this, but if they are truly novel, they will still embody some element of design, function, or utility that is unique and proprietary. If it really is 'novel,' then by definition it has never been done before—and if it has never been done before, it is reasonable for a potential licensee to have doubts as to your ability to do it. More to the point, since most people are pretty much dullards in these matters, if something has never been done before, they will basically assume it can't be done. That is why we, as inventors, have such a vast realm of opportunity and potential; and why we build breadboards that we can put in front of these people and say, "see, you jackass—I told you it would work!"

And that is why it is very important to have a demonstrable breadboard of the key aspect of even relatively simple inventions.

Hands-on

Breadboards serve a crucial function beyond just demonstrating the viability of the concept. A breadboard is a crucible in which the practicality and viability of your invention is tested. In your head, every idea is great and there are never any contradictions, inadequacies, logical inconsistencies, or physical impossibilities. It's easy to forget about things like the laws of physics or the properties of materials or the interference of two components which have to occupy the same space at the same time. But reality—in the guise of a breadboard is not nearly so forgiving. Once you begin to reduce your invention to practice, the harsh light of reality quickly highlights any mistakes, oversights, or misconceptions on your part. And this is not a bad thing. If you hope to eventually have a viable commercial product, you need to discover any problems right away and do whatever is necessary to correct them.

I have often found that building the first (or second or twentieth) breadboard is where I really understand what my invention is all about—and this is why I believe that it is critical that you do this work yourself. Even if you have no tools and no technical or mechanical experience, dig in and try to make something. It doesn't have to be pretty, and it doesn't have to look like a product; but if you take the time to think about what components are needed, and how they can be assembled to work cooperatively, you will gain valuable insights into the essence of your invention.

Chewing gum and paperclips

Breadboarding is all about resourcefulness. Since you aren't trying to win a prize for how beautiful your breadboard is, and since you may end up throwing it away and starting over again, it makes perfect sense to build it as inexpensively and expeditiously as possible. Get creative with your choice of materials and methods. I have used modeling clay to sculpt a part which ultimately needed to be machined out of steel, just so I could check size and shape and geometry assumptions I had made. No need to pay a machine shop for that. I frequently use 'paper dolls'—cut outs of components to test the 2 dimensional relationships or fit of parts, before I go to the time, trouble and expense of building more representative three dimensional parts. This can be a great tool for checking out simple mechanisms—

for example if you need some part of your invention to fold or telescope or slide into or around some other part—cut out paper profiles of the parts and pin them to a piece of cardboard to simulate pivot points and start moving things around. It's amazing what you can learn from such a simple exercise; and you can save a lot of time and money by avoiding mistakes on more expensive 'real' parts.

The greatest value of the breadboard

The single most important contribution of the breadboard is solidifying your understanding of your invention to the point that you can protect your idea (file a patent application) with the confidence that you have worked out all of the major issues. One of the tests that an invention must pass in order to be considered patentable is that of 'practicality'—which means that you have to demonstrate how the invention can be 'reduced to practice' or in lay terms— show how to make one which actually works.

It is a big mistake to file a patent application before you have reduced your invention to practice or breadboarded it, because you will invariably find that you missed something or left out a vital design consideration, necessitating re-filing your patent application.

Paying for it

One of the great challenges of developing an invention is figuring out how to pay for the sometimes considerable costs associated with creating, prototyping, machining, molding, patenting, marketing, or producing your product. There are plenty of good books about how to raise money out there, so I won't go into a lot of detail here, other than to say that most people have plenty of options if you get a little bit creative—savings, family, friends, business associates, investors, etc. There are two things to be careful of when asking people for money: first, any 'solicitation for investment' is considered a 'public offering' in the eyes of the Securities and Exchange Commission (SEC) so you want to make sure you know what you're doing before you post an ad in the local paper asking for money in exchange for ownership in your company or invention. This is quite illegal and can put you in a rather sticky situation. Second, you want to really think through the whole notion of having 'partners' in your business. Remember—it's really easy to ask people for money and give them a stake in your company or product; but they are there for a long, long time and it can be a real pain in the ass to have to deal with people who don't like the way you are running your company or don't feel like they are seeing an adequate return on their investment. Sometimes it's better to figure out how to pay for it yourself or do without than to end up in bed with partners who are less than ideal.

A new model for raising money has been developed recently which is quite promising—'crowd funding.' Companies like Kickstarter and Indiegogo among others allow inventors to post detailed descriptions of their projects along with specific capital requirements and 'rewards' for donors in order to raise necessary money. You can't offer stock in your company or repayment of any investment, but you can offer sample products or autographed pictures or anything else that might be of value and interest. The best part is—you don't end up with 'partners' and you don't have to pay back the money. Of course prospective donors have lots and lots of choices for what to invest in, so you will need to make sure that your project is appealing. Another benefit of 'crowd funding' is the informal focus group or consumer feedback you get. Obviously, if nobody funds it, you probably need to re-think whether your invention has any appeal. But you can also solicit suggestions for design changes or product modifications or enhancements to make sure your invention will be appealing to a broad audience. The obvious caveat to these 'crowd funding' vehicles is the 'publication' or public disclosure of your invention as part of the solicitation process. It would be prudent to take measures to protect your idea before this kind of broad and unrestricted disclosure.

Step Three: Protecting Your Idea

It is vital that you understand how to protect your invention through the use of Confidential Disclosure Agreements, Submission Agreements, Patents, Copyrights, Trade Marks, or Trade Secrets. There are actually two entirely separate issues here. The first relates to keeping your invention confidential, private, or secret, and the second involves defining and establishing your legal rights to defend your invention from those who would steal it or copy it.

The importance of confidentiality

By now, it should be fairly apparent why you need to use a Confidential Disclosure Agreement when presenting your idea to a potential licensee (or even to your neighbor for that matter). The agreement creates a legally binding relationship between you and whoever you share your invention with that protects the confidentiality of your intellectual property. Obviously, if you didn't take steps to protect your inventions, anybody who got wind of them could go out and license or manufacture them on their own and not pay you a cent. Unlike being a baker where the product you sell is cakes and you just keep making more of them to sell, when you are an inventor, the only thing you have to sell is your ideas and you need to take precautions to keep them secret and protect their commercial value.

The other reason you have to carefully define the terms under which you allow someone to review your ideas is that it is very likely that the first (and possibly the second, third, fourth ad infinitum) entity you share them with will not be the one with which you ultimately sign a license agreement. When you finally do make a deal with someone, they will want (and are certainly entitled to receive) every assurance from you that the idea is indeed novel and proprietary. If you have been sloppy and shown your invention to individuals or corporations without the appropriate legal agreements in place, you may well have jeopardized your invention's confidentiality, and therefore commercial viability.

Publication

Intellectual property law defines any non-confidential disclosure idea of your idea to the 'public' (and this can be one person behind locked conference room doors in a privately held corporation, or it can be what we usually understand as 'the public'), wherein you demonstrate your invention or offer it for commercial sale—as "publication." As a matter of genuine practical importance, if you "publish" your invention prior to filing for patent protection, particularly foreign patents, you may risk forfeiting the ability to obtain patent protection at all, or possibly start the clock on a time constrained period during which you must file in order to secure protection.

So this brings us to the subject of patents—probably the most widely and consistently misunderstood aspect of the invention business. What is a patent, what is it good for, how do you get one, and should you bother? All critical questions, the answers to which you must fully understand before you can operate knowledgeably, safely, comfortably, and profitably in the intellectual property development game.

What is a patent?

Of course you've heard of patents, and you probably even have a pretty good idea what they are, right? Wrong. Contrary to what you may believe or may have heard, a patent is *not* a license to make or sell a product. It is *not* something you must, or even *should* have in order to sell an invention. And finally, a patent *certainly doesn't* guarantee that you can or will make any money.

So what the hell is a patent then? Here is the actual definition of a patent from the United States Patent and Trademark Office:

"A patent is a type of property right. It gives the patent holder, for a period of time, the right to exclude others from making, using, offering to sell, selling, or importing into the United States the subject matter that is within the scope of the protection of the patent. The

USPTO determines whether a patent should be granted in a particular case. However, it is up to the patent holder to enforce his or her own rights if the USPTO does grant a patent."

What exactly does that mean? Very simply, a patent is a document which gives you the right to take legal action to prevent a third party from making, using, selling, or importing products which infringe on your patent, within the country in which the patent is issued and recognized (you can apply for patents in most countries in the world, not just the United States).

That's it? Yes, that's it. A patent just gives you a legal basis for suing somebody. It doesn't guarantee you will win. It doesn't guarantee you will be compensated by the party you are suing for stealing your idea; and it absolutely doesn't mean that the government or some kind hearted lawyer is going to pick up the tab for the cost of litigation.

Do you need a patent?

So if a patent is nothing more than the right to sue somebody, do you really need to go to all of the time, trouble and expense to get one? It pretty much comes down to one issue: do you intend to commercialize your invention yourself, or do you intend to license it to a large manufacturer/marketer? If you plan on commercializing it yourself, and you are not immensely wealthy, odds are good that you would be ill-advised to seek a patent given the fact that you would likely not be able to afford to defend it. If, on the other hand, you are going to attempt to license your invention to a large company, you should definitely attempt to secure as strong a patent as possible because this will in large part dictate the value of the invention to the company. The broader and stronger the patent, the more valuable and defensible the 'temporary monopoly' it grants to the entity which controls it—so it becomes both safer and more reasonable for that entity to invest large amounts of money to secure, develop and promote the invention without fear of being knocked off or undercut by a potential competitor (in a legal fashion—of course if someone infringes, they have armies of lawyers just champing at the bit to go after them). Since your license fee and royalty arrangement are part of the 'investment' a company makes in an invention, it stands to reason that the better protected the invention, the more money you can expect to receive for it.

A patent is simply a ticket to launch a lawsuit, and as a result it is both fair and accurate to say that the *value of a patent is directly proportional to the willingness and ability of the controlling party to prosecute anyone who infringes it.* Stated another way, the value of a patent is proportional to the depth of the pockets and the robustness of the constitution of the party that controls it. You could have the strongest patent in the world, but people will infringe it and walk all over you if you don't have the resources or inclination to sue them to make them stop. This is a nontrivial point. Patent litigation is some of the costliest and ugliest legal wrangling you can imagine. It is not only easy to ring up a legal bill in the hundreds of thousands or millions of dollars; it is likely that any litigation will stretch out over many years— so even if you do ultimately prevail, you will have spent a huge sum of money in the process. Patent litigation is a game for the big boys and would-be infringers know this. History is filled with examples of big companies or wealthy people who brazenly infringed patents based solely on the knowledge that they could out-spend and out-last the patent holder if they challenged the infringement in court. Watch the movie "Flash of Genius" for a real-life example of just how costly patent litigation can be.

Okay, that's the worst of it—we now understand that a patent doesn't give you the ability or legal right to sell your product—so it seems reasonable to say that you don't really need a patent to make money from your invention, right? Well, if you do not have the money or litigious nature to sue people left and right the minute they even think about infringing your patent, then yes, you're probably right—not only don't you need a patent—you'd most likely be wasting your time and money applying for one.

But it's unlikely that you will be the one commercializing your invention. It's much more likely to be marketed by a mid to large sized company with both the resources and the inclination to litigate—*but more importantly, they will have a very big investment to protect.* Remember our earlier discussion about everything that's involved in taking an invention to market—how it becomes a product through engineering and tooling and testing and certification, and all of the other expenses relating to manufacturing and packaging and marketing and insuring and shipping and more? Well, no company in their right mind is going to invest all of the time, money, and resources required to do this if they don't have some assurance that they will see a return on their investment—and the only way they'll see a return is if their position in the marketplace is protected in some way. Or to put it another way, they will want to have a limited monopoly which will give them a period of time to market their product without competition, during which time they can recoup their investment and make a profit—kinda sounds like the definition of a patent, doesn't it?

Remember the widget maker who worries every day that someone is going to come out with a widget that's a little cheaper and a lot better? That's because our widgeteer is in *an unprotected position in a commodity marketplace.* He has no proprietary advantages to distinguish his products from everyone else's, so he is totally exposed to this sort of undercutting. And when he spends lots of money advertising and marketing his widgets, and you and I walk into the store to buy one but pick up the generic competitor's product right next to his because we can save a nickel—he loses out big time.

If, on the other hand, this guy's widgets are the ones with some juicy, irresistible proprietary feature that we just can't live without, when we walk into the store to buy one we'll take one look at the cheap knock-offs and turn up our noses. Who would want that inferior piece of crap? It doesn't have the (fill in the blank with some must-have proprietary feature)! And how did this widget become so wonderfully irresistible? Because a smart, charming inventor type like you came up with a great idea and licensed it to the guy—revitalizing his business and making a nice chunk of change for himself every time a widget sells.

But let's say this "king of the widget world" guy is a bit spineless and wimpy. And let's say some unscrupulous competitor decides to copy his product exactly—but sell it for less. He can *afford* to sell it for less because he doesn't have to pay an inventor a royalty, and he doesn't have to do all of that expensive development and engineering work—he just straight-up copies it. Right away his sales are going to go through the roof. He'll be going like gangbusters. And if our mild mannered widget king doesn't get off the fence and sick at least a couple of four hundred dollar an hour lawyers on this fellow, his own sales will likely plummet and he'll end up going out of business. And that's precisely what a patent enables you to do and why it is a good thing to have.

Let's think about this some more—is it really the ability to sue somebody that makes patents important? It's actually much more than this—it is the concept of the *temporary monopoly* which a patent conveys that makes it so valuable.

But I thought that monopolies are bad, and hurt competition and drive up prices?

The truth is exactly the opposite—the temporary monopoly is nothing more than a protected haven—a brief respite for a manufacturer where he can sell his proprietary products without fear of being knocked off. Why is this so important? Because as we have seen, it is really difficult, risky, time consuming and expensive to come up with new products, and the newer they are, the more revolutionary, the bigger the advantage they convey generally speaking, the more difficult, time consuming and expensive they are to bring to market. And since our culture, and the progress, stability and well-being of our country depend on a steady flow of innovation, we have to do everything we can to facilitate and encourage it.

Absent any protections, it is clear that the innovator not only fails to benefit fully from his efforts and investments—he is actually at a considerable disadvantage. If one company invests all of the money in research and development, licensing, tooling, and marketing to establish a great new product and the requisite consumer awareness to drive sales, and another company just comes along and knocks this product off and sells it at a much lower price because their costs are lower, without fear of consequences, we impose a strong disincentive in the marketplace to be an innovator, or to be the first to introduce a new product. Since what we want is precisely the opposite—we want to incentivise innovation and ongoing evolutionary developments—we have devised the system of patent protection which gives an innovator not only a brief protected period to recoup his investment, or financially 'catch his breath' as it were, but the gift of a relatively short period of total domination of a narrow segment of the marketplace. Think of it as a mini-monopoly; and think of this mini-monopoly as the carrot we dangle in front of individual inventors and corporations to entice them to take the risks necessary to foster a steady stream of innovation which will benefit us all.

And there is yet another layer of motivation and incentivisation that takes place—not only doesn't this mini-monopoly throw a wet blanket on the competitive fires burning in the hearts of the competition—it *stokes* them. If they feel as though they have been painted into a corner by their competitor's proprietary advances, they will assuredly redouble their efforts to come up with their own. It is capitalism at its most basic—greed and the desire to dominate one's competition as a primal and powerful economic engine.

So patents can be powerful assets; but they are not

always necessary. There are a number of scenarios to consider where the time, money and energy required to file for and prosecute a patent is likely unnecessary: the highly volatile world of seasonal products or 'one hit wonders.' In certain industries such as the toy industry or the fashion industry, the useful commercial life of a new product can be as little as one selling season, or about 4 months. These are both industries with an enormous appetite for the 'latest and greatest,' or at least something new and different. It is not at all uncommon to get one Christmas selling season out of a toy and then it's done. It's the same with certain fashion accessories. It can be a very fickle and volatile business. In these situations, given that it can take several years for a patent application to be prosecuted and ultimately issue, it is clearly a case of closing the barn door well after the cows have all gone. The key to success in these scenarios is the speed and efficiency with which one can get through the development and manufacturing cycle and get products on the shelves in stores. By the time the competition realizes that you've created an opportunity which they should attempt to knock off, it has vanished into thin air. If you are in this kind of highly volatile industry, feel free to say, "patents, schmatents" because they are essentially irrelevant.

The one caveat to all of this is that you never know when that 'flash in the pan' or 'one hit wonder' is going to become a big hit with staying power—and if this staying power drags across multiple selling seasons or several years, or best of all, if the product becomes what is known in the retail business as an 'evergreen' or staple item which sells consistently season after season, year after year, you are now at great peril of being knocked off. If the possibility exists that this situation could develop (and what inventor doesn't hope for such a thing?), you would be well advised to at the very least file a provisional patent application which gives you a year to figure out if filing a non-provisional application and going to the time, trouble, and expense of prosecuting it is warranted.

One final scenario in which a patent may be unnecessary is where you are simply too small of a target for anyone to bother with. 'Small target' doesn't simply mean low volume—if you sell one nuclear reactor a year for $100 billion with a fifty percent profit margin, you'll likely feel the hounds nipping at your heels. But if you sell a small number of low priced, modestly profitable items, it's hardly incentive enough for the would-be knock off artists to take aim at you. There are many such scenarios— you might have come up with a nifty invention which helps with your specialized job or hobby— say a clamp which makes the hitherto onerous task of holding a gerbil's legs apart while you surgically castrate it-- and you can sell a dozen or so to your gaggle of buddies with similar proclivities—you are not what we in the industry refer to as a 'high value target.' Of course the same caveat applies here as it did above—what if your 'little' invention takes off and becomes the next big thing? A provisional patent application will give you one year to make the determination as to whether more substantial protection is necessary or worthwhile.

More reasons to get a patent

We've talked about plenty of reasons why you may not need a patent, but there are plenty more why you do: first, they make a darned nice looking plaque hanging on the wall of your home office. Seriously— many people are happy to get a patent just so they can display it proudly as a symbol of their brains or entrepreneurial acumen. Bully for them. Not the best reason in the world to go to the trouble and expense, but to each his own.

Another reason is a slightly more legitimate form of 'showing off.' Companies, or start-ups, or individuals attempting to raise capital to commercialize an invention will oftentimes attempt to secure patent protection as a way of 'proving' or legitimizing the value of their undertaking. Presumably the logic has something to do with the notion that a patent is tangible proof that someone has done something. Fortunately for most who attempt to utilize patents in this way, the vast majority of the population has no idea what a patent really is or how to evaluate the merits of any individual patent, so this ruse can be quite effective. It is certainly true that a patent is evidence that someone has done something, but in the vast majority of cases it establishes simply that an ill-informed person wasted a lot of time and money.

Another reason to seek out a patent is to establish value for a business. Intellectual property is a business asset in precisely the same way that a building or a machine or a pallet of finished goods is. While establishing the precise worth of a patent is a bit of a slippery subject, there is no question but that the ownership of a patent does add value to a company's balance sheet. It is also an asset which may be leveraged in a sale of a business; and there have been many cases where the only value calculated for a business has been the intellectual property it controlled.

Additionally, many companies seek out patents not

to proactively pursue infringers, but to establish a robust defensive posture. A patent can clearly and objectively 'stake out' a company's 'turf' in the sense that it explicitly defines the boundaries of the intellectual property it controls, and by inference, the products it can commercialize. In the event that a more litigious competitor wishes to challenge this company's position or carve out a piece of its 'turf,' there is no better defense than the control of a patent which states in black and white what that turf is, and what that turf isn't.

Finally, there has been a trend recently where highly litigious individuals or entities acquire patents for the express purpose of suing companies who market products which knowingly or unknowingly infringe them. This is the worst sort of use of patents, but it is an unfortunately growing trend which has made huge sums of money for the aggressors— in some cases because they have been awarded large amounts by a judge or jury, and in more cases because it is cheaper for a defendant in such a suit to write a big check to settle rather than spending millions defending the charges. I hope that this abuse of the patent system is examined and remedied in the near future because it is having precisely the opposite effect on the marketplace than what was intended—it is stifling innovation and causing truly creative, entrepreneurial companies and individuals to hesitate to invest in new products because of a fear of having to pay 'ransom' in order to do business.

A warning about the advice of patent attorneys

Patent attorneys come in all sizes, shapes, and degrees of competence, but having worked with a large number of them, I've noticed a disturbing trend. Most (competent) patent attorneys are good at assessing the merits of an invention, particularly with regard to distinctions over prior art, and thereby effectively crafting a patent to secure the broadest possible protections for the inventor. In so doing, they attempt to insure that the inventor will have the legal right to pursue anyone who attempts to copy his invention. While it might seem that this is the essence of the job of a patent lawyer, this is actually only one of three really important basic functions that the patent attorney should be performing for his client. The second is an assessment of the likelihood that the inventor's patent will infringe somebody else's patent and the strategic positioning of the invention which will allow it a 'clear shot' or infringement-free market opportunity.

This is another one of those profoundly misunderstood aspects of patent law—just because you have been granted a patent, there is no assurance that you can commercialize a product based on that patent without infringing someone else's intellectual property. In fact, it is not only possible to obtain a patent on an invention which cannot be commercialized without infringing one or more existing patents, it is fairly likely. This is a phenomenon which is well understood by professionals, and most patent attorneys are pretty good at this step as well.

But there is a third piece of the puzzle which is arguably the most important of them all, yet curiously seems to escape most patent attorneys. To review, the first function of the patent development process should be a determination of the potential scope of the proposed patent—or how well the invention in question can be protected which is directly related to its value in the marketplace; while the second is a determination of the likelihood of infringing someone else's patents—both important steps to be sure, but far from comprehensive in the evaluation and protection of the commercial viability of an invention. The third and potentially most important (and frequently neglected) piece is an assessment of the opportunities potential competitors might avail themselves of to capitalize on the consumer awareness and demand you've created with your invention, without infringing on your patent. What I mean is this—let's suppose your patent attorney has done a bang up job crafting a patent application which quite thoroughly covers your invention with the intention of preventing anyone from copying your idea and stealing your thunder. On top of this, he has analyzed the prior art and determined that you can commercialize your invention without infringing anybody else's patents. Great, right? Not so great—for a number of reasons. First, patenting your specific invention may give you only very narrow protection—meaning someone might be able to come up with a variation or subtle change and no longer fall under the scope of protection of your patent. So in order to prevent this, it is important that the patent be as broad as possible and contemplate every possible combination and permutation of features, constructions, materials, etc. And even if you end up with a reasonably broad patent which covers many variations of your invention, it likely still fails to consider fundamentally different ways of solving the same problem. What I mean is this: if you come up with a great invention which solves a known problem, and then you do a great job of not only creating consumer awareness and demand, but also secure a strong patent on that invention, if your competition comes up with a completely different way of solving the same problem (which does not have anything to do with your invention and doesn't infringe your patent), then the value of your invention is quite limited—because it doesn't give you a protected position in the marketplace. To put it another way, if one or more competitors can sell to the same consumers as you, in response to the same needs, without infringing your patent—then your patent does nothing to protect your position and therefore has very little value. So how do you prevent this from happening? Remember our discussion about how important it is to avoid 'falling in love' with your invention? How you have to keep an open mind and not be blinded by the brilliance of your solution? It's all about focusing on the opportunity rather than any particular solution. You have to put your invention aside and think about every other possible way of solving the same problem. And you have to include these solutions in your patent application. In this way you can insure that not only will you bring to market the very best of many possible solutions; but more importantly you will have considered every possible angle from which a prospective competitor could launch an attack.

This approach of envisioning and protecting multiple solutions to the same problem and seeking patent protection for all of them builds what is known as an "estate of intellectual property" around your core idea. The goal is to stake out a wide buffer zone of defensible space surrounding your central invention, in order to ward off would-be competitors.

Here's the bottom line: patents are basically a legal tool which can be a powerful resource to protect your 'limited monopoly' in the marketplace. If you have made the decision that you want to avail yourself of these tools, you might as well make sure that the tools are effective. And in order to be effective, a patent has to not only protect your invention, and insure that you can market your invention without getting sued by somebody else, but most importantly it has to insure that nobody can solve the same problem without being subject to your legal remedies.

If a patent does not create a protected position in the marketplace (which means you are the only person who can sell a product which solves a particular problem), it has limited to no value.

There is one more potential pitfall to be aware of as you contemplate and construct your patent protection strategy: covering your invention thoroughly with one or more patents does nothing to prevent someone from commercializing a variation of the invention covered by an existing patent whether active or expired. Think of it this way—you come up with an idea which you disclose to your patent attorney. He does a patent search and informs you that there are a few related patents but no 'dead ringers' out there—you're looking at a couple of expired patents (now in the public domain), and a few active patents which are minor improvements on the basic concept. He explains that it is his opinion that you can get a strong patent to cover your invention because it is clearly a novel improvement over the basic concept, and distinct from the inventions disclosed in the active patents. Great—so you spend lots of money and time and get your patent application filed, then spend even more money and time developing, engineering, tooling, and manufacturing your product, and still more time and money building a company to sell it, and yet more money advertising and promoting it to create market awareness and demand. Just when you have a nice buzz going in the marketplace and it seems like you've got the hottest new product ever, you are deeply chagrined to see a cheap knockoff introduced which steals 80% of the market share. Well—if that's how they're going to play, you'll simply have to exercise your legal rights and sue the bastards for patent infringement, right? So what if it will cost a million bucks and take ten years—it's worth it to defend your empire.

Oops, wait a minute—that cheap knock-off doesn't actually infringe your patent—it's based on the teachings of one of the expired, public domain patents—or worse, one of those active patents your attorney carefully navigated around to avoid infringement issues with your invention.

The moral of the story? Make sure you have considered every possible approach to solving a problem—especially those approaches which you cannot control (because they are covered by prior art, or are in the public domain) in order to realistically assess the true commercial value and potential of your invention. And once you have a solid objective grasp on what the opportunity is, you may have to file several different patent applications to carve out a sufficiently large piece of the turf. The bottom line is this-- make sure you determine how much damage a potential competitor could do by marketing a product based on prior art whether active or public domain, before putting all of your eggs in one basket.

An alternative to patents

So we see that a patent can be a powerful tool for cultivating and protecting a new market segment for proprietary products; but this is entirely dependent upon an aggressive defense of one's legal rights accorded thereunder on the part of the patent holder, and a respect for these rights on the part of the wolves circling at the door. This begs the question "what if I don't want to spend hundreds of thousands or millions of dollars suing everybody and then have to wait for ten years for the case to be adjudicated? What are my other options?" Basically, there are two options for protecting your proprietary product which can be used instead of patent protection. The first is based on an understanding of why products get 'knocked off.'

If you make a completely uninteresting product which is selling for a rock bottom price with barely any profit margin, nobody is going to come in and try to steal your market share away from you. If, however, you have just introduced the hottest new product on TV and you're making money hand over fist, you can bet that you will have knock offs hitting the shelves within days. What's the difference between the two examples? The fundamental difference is the perception of a 'window of opportunity' which exists for the successful product. By coming up with something new which has generated strong consumer interest and is very profitable, you have created a vacuum in the marketplace which will suck in all of the opportunists who will try to get a piece of the action. You have done all of the hard work—you have come up with something innovative, you have created consumer demand, and you have made one crucial mistake—you established price points which leave plenty of room for profit.

So how do you defend against the onslaught if you don't have patent rights to support your lawsuits? You *close* the 'window of opportunity,' or at the very least you make it much smaller. An opportunity which is smaller will be less attractive and draw fewer would-be competitors. Closing this window is as simple as evaluating where you stand with respect to the three best positions to occupy in the marketplace according to classical marketing theory, and trying to commandeer all of them—the first, the best, and the least expensive.

Aren't these three positions mutually exclusive? Not at all—you are probably the *first* already, so you have that covered. If, instead of rushing your products out into the market, you do your homework and thoughtfully and meticulously design and engineer them for optimal appearance, performance, utility, and value, you can easily be the best in the market as well. And if you price your products fairly, perhaps even aggressively, you can come close enough to being the *cheapest* that the incentive is gone for the wolves to move in and try to sink their teeth into those big, juicy profits. It doesn't mean that you can't make money—it means that you can't be sloppy or gross about it. Pigs get fat, hogs get slaughtered. Even if you have the world's strongest patent, you could spend the next twenty years of your life as well as the better part of all of your profits trying to ward off the infringers if you market a product which is initially successful in spite of its being somewhat poorly designed and overpriced—and therefore a tempting target for the knock off guys.

A well designed innovative product at an aggressive price point is the best defense against would be knock off competitors—close the 'window of opportunity' and nobody will jump through it.

You know you've done everything right when a would be competitor picks up your product and analyzes it admiringly, then shakes his head and says, "how the hell are they selling this thing at this price and making any money?"

A second approach to protecting your proprietary product from would-be knock off artists is the use of 'trade secrets.' Bear in mind that once a patent is issued, it is now accessible to anybody for scrutiny and review. Basically, when your patent issues, you are telling the world—"this is exactly how I'm doing my magic, and these are the features that are proprietary, and these are the features that I can't protect and pretty much anybody can copy, and these are the limits of my turf, so if you can figure out a way to get around me, have at it." It's a little bit scary—you're really laying your cards on the table and showing the competition exactly what you've got. The alternative is to not file for a patent and rely on 'trade secrets' or the confidentiality of precisely how you do whatever it is you do that makes your product proprietary. This might be a secret recipe, or a secret formulation, or a secret program in a computer chip—but the operative term here is 'secret.' If the secret gets out, you're done for—you have no fall back position. Once the competition knows your secrets, they can do precisely what you are doing and you can't stop them. And they can very likely sell for less because they don't have the development costs to recoup or royalties to pay. Obviously, you would only opt for this route if you felt you had a pretty good chance of keeping your secrets *secret*— meaning they are not easily discerned or 'reverse-engineered' (copied).

A variation on the 'trade secret' approach is just

keeping your product hushed up until it actually hits the store shelves. If there's a whole bunch of publicity and brouhaha months or years before you're ready to start selling, you give your dishonest competitors all of the time they need to knock you off—sometimes their copies hit the shelves even before you get into the market. But if you are able to keep a lid on it until you're actually selling, this may give you enough of a head start in the marketplace that your competitors never catch up—especially if it's a 'one season' type of product. Even if someone decides to knock off your product on the very first day it hits the shelves, they will have several months of copying, tooling, production and transportation/distribution to contend with. Sometimes that 'couple of months' head start is all you need to make your splash—you get in and make your money, then get out before it gets too crowded or ugly.

Patent pending

Wouldn't it be great if there was a way of securing all of the protections and advantages of a patent without having to disclose every intimate detail of your invention to the whole world—to be able to keep it secret? Well, there is just such a beast. It can only be done for a relatively short time, but it may keep the wolves at bay just long enough to get your product to market, make all of your money, and get out—and it's called "patent pending." Technically, 'patent pending' means that the United States Patent and Trademark Office acknowledges that you have submitted an application for a patent, and their office has not yet issued a patent based on this application. Having 'patent pending' status gives absolutely no indication as to whether or not a patent will ever be issued, or if it does issue, how strong it will be or whether it will infringe other patents. 'Patent Pending' literally means that the USPTO has received your application for a patent. Nothing more, nothing less. This status, however, can have some distinct advantages.

A patent application is a fairly involved document which includes a very detailed disclosure of your invention and a whole bunch of paperwork you submit to the patent office in the hopes of getting a patent. Anyone who gets to review this material will have a complete understanding of exactly what your invention is and is not; and what if anything will be covered by your patent, if it ever issues. One of the critical distinctions between a patent application and an issued patent is that the Patent Office keeps patent applications confidential (for a period of time), while they publish issued patents for unrestricted review. This period of secrecy can be a much stronger deterrent to would be competitors than having an issued patent. Why? Because first of all, until the patent issues and becomes publicly available, the competition has no idea that you are 'up to something' let alone exactly what you're doing. If they catch wind of the fact that you're going to be introducing a new product and they want to develop a competitive product, if they have even the slightest respect for patent rights, or any fear of patent litigation for infringement, they will very likely hold off on creating their product until they are fairly certain just what is going to be covered by your patent—because if they go ahead and invest in something which turns out to infringe your patent, they stand to lose everything. But once your patent issues and they can study it and see exactly where the 'holes' are in your coverage, or figure out how they can get around your patent without infringing, you have lost the benefit of 'potential coverage' as is implied when you have patent pending status.

Once you have filed your patent application and received acknowledgment from the patent office that they have received your application, you may legally label your product 'patent pending.' And the great part is, even if your patent application is flimsy or you stand no chance of ever getting a meaningful patent issued, you are allowed to label your product as 'patent pending' and take full advantage of the benefits and protections, and even 'scare tactics' this status provides. And since it usually takes *at least* two years, and sometimes longer, for the patent office to give even the first response to your patent application, you can wear that appellation for quite a while.

So in a way, a 'patent pending' label is a bit of a straw man—you go out into the marketplace waving your big red flag that says 'patent pending' trying to scare off any would-be competitors, even if your patent position is actually very weak. But it may be enough of a perceived risk or obstacle on the part of the competition that they'll give you the breathing room you need to make your big splash. Many products only have a one or two 'season' life cycle anyhow (like fashion items or gimmicky toys) so a little head start is oftentimes all you need to fully capture and exploit the market. Of course, the more 'breathing room,' or the longer the unchallenged competitive advantage you have, the better off you will be.

Breathing room

That 'breathing room' concept is an important aspect of the commercial value of patents. While the 'patent pending' period may be the most useful or desirable, it is important to understand that once a patent finally *does* issue, it is good for a non-renewable, non-extendable period of twenty years (fourteen years for a design patent)—and the clock starts as of the *filing* date, not the issue date. So make hay while the sun shines. At the end of the life of the patent (on the day it expires), your brilliant little proprietary invention becomes public domain property—it now belongs to the world—and anyone can do anything they want with it. If you are the patent holder, this is a scary thought. If you are an inventor looking for an opportunity to sell a new proprietary angle to a soon-to-be-commodity product manufacturer, this is a big opportunity.

Types of patents

Let's talk a little bit more about the different kinds of patents and what you have to do to get one. There are basically three kinds of patents: utility patents, design patents and something called 'plant' patents (which are for genetically engineered plants). We're really only talking about utility patents here because I'm not engineering any plants any time soon; and design patents are for the most part worthless. I know a lot of people are going to get upset by this, but it's a simple truth—a design patent really has no commercial value and can't prevent a single person from marketing a directly competitive product—it just protects your very specific 'ornamental design' for your product. Big deal. If you have come up with some incredible new gizmo and all you have is a design patent protecting it, every competitor in the world will figure out a way to make that gizmo look *slightly* different and, bingo, they're in the gizmo business with no fear of infringement lawsuits.

To be fair, design patents can be very important and valuable for companies who have built and are trying to protect their brand based on a specific ornamental appearance of their products. Basically, the design patent gives you the legal right to sue someone to prevent them from making or selling products which look more or less exactly like yours—

or which could easily be mistaken for yours. So the design patent has a very different purpose than the utility patent—it is about preventing 'look-alikes' rather than protecting a solution to a problem.

Breadth of coverage

What we care about are utility patents. A utility patent covers the functional aspects of an invention—obviously this is a much stronger degree of protection than a design patent. But what most people don't realize is that *a utility patent can range in protection from being very strong to being functionally worthless.* How can this be? It all comes down to a concept known as 'breadth of coverage.' Basically this amounts to how wide a net your patent casts over the general field of interest in which your invention resides. In other words, if you invent a pencil and you get a patent which covers "hand held implements employing graphite or lead to create markings"—you have an amazingly broad and strong patent. If, on the other hand, you end up with a patent which covers "an implement to be held in the left hand of right handed people which is bluish-green in color, precisely 5.3 inches long, precisely .237 inches in diameter, with a yellow eraser at one end and a point at the other which must be an angle of exactly 22.3 degrees, and containing a graphite material of a composition known by the commercial name "Uncle Louie's Cheapo Pencil Lead," which also has a small image of a purple kangaroo on the body, exactly halfway between the point and the eraser"—you are now the proud owner of a hard-fought, rather expensive, worthless piece of paper. The first patent more or less excludes anybody from selling anything which even remotely resembles a pencil. The second patent could be gotten around by a blind monkey throwing darts at a list of adjectives. The problem with the second patent is that it is much too specific. The more general the language of a patent, and the fewer conditions, specific terms, or caveats—the broader and stronger it is.

But where in the patent does one find the language (describing the invention) that really matters? It is in a section of the patent known as the 'claims.' Here is where you clearly articulate and define the limits of, or *claim*, exactly what it is about your invention that is novel in the simplest, broadest terms possible. *Generally speaking-- the simpler the language, the fewer modifiers, adjectives, adverbs, or qualifiers there are, and the shorter the sentences in the claims, the stronger the patent.*

Your patented invention may still infringe

It is time to point out one of the great misconceptions of patents and intellectual property law—even if you own a strong patent, you may not be able to manufacture or sell your invention without infringing somebody else's patent. How is this possible? Because the standard that the patent office applies in evaluating an invention to determine if it is worthy of a patent is this—"is it novel, is it useful, and is it non-obvious to one skilled in the art?" The novel and useful parts are more or less self-explanatory, so let's just look at the 'non-obvious to one skilled in the art' bit. This means that a person who is generally knowledgeable about the particular field in which this invention exists would not find the improvements suggested by the inventor to be 'obvious.' For example, if the patent application describes a liquid crystal display with a photo-etched indium tin oxide layer which has been deposited in an unusually thick layer to permit higher current signals to be used to collapse the helix of the media, most lay people would read this and say, "this has got to be a brilliant invention—I don't understand a word of it!" But to one skilled in the art, varying the thickness of the ITO layer is not only obvious, it's fairly inane—as liquid crystal molecules respond to potential differences, or voltage, rather than current. Unless the inventor demonstrates that there is a fundamental new utility here—a new way of addressing the molecules for example, this application gets rejected on the basis of being obvious. But let's say our not-so-smart inventor actually got a patent for his thick ITO layer. Great—now all he has to do is start selling these new displays and make a fortune, right? Not so fast there genius—just because you lucked out and got a patent for a relatively minor improvement to the fabrication details of a liquid crystal display doesn't mean you now have the right to manufacture or sell the entire display. You will very likely be stepping on many toes, and infringing many patents if you try to sell one display. The best you can hope for is to find a company who already controls (owns or has licensed) the fundamental patents relating to liquid crystal displays, and license them your pitiful little invention. The key lesson to take from this is—*just because you obtained a patent, it does not guarantee that you can make or sell your invention without infringing other people's patents.*

Patent law is no hobby

The claims are really the most important part of a patent to understand; but there are many other fascinating and arcane details that go into making up a patent which you should make it your business to become familiar with. To this end, I would encourage you to read through as many patents as possible to try and get a sense of what they contain, how they are worded, and what is and is not included. A very good place to start is the United States Patent and Trademark Office official website which is at www. uspto.gov. You will find that spending some time wandering around the site will yield invaluable insights into the world of patents as well as prepare you to do some of your own novelty searches (which we'll discuss shortly).

But probably the first thing you'll notice is that the language, organization, and logic of a patent is a bizarre thing indeed. The secret language of patents— the parlance and vernacular of intellectual property is a dialect that no human being has ever employed, save patent lawyers. Read through a bunch of patents and you'll start to get the hang of it; but be advised—comprehending a patent is not the same thing as being competent or qualified to draft one-- crafting the specific language and organization of patents is a highly specialized skill which is best left to professionals. It is certainly true that you *could* prepare and prosecute your own patent application, but odds are quite good that you will be doing your invention and yourself a disservice in so doing. What's that line about the man who represents himself having a fool for a client?

The patent process

So even if we concede the actual business of preparing a patent application to the pros, it's still worthwhile spending a little time talking about how the whole process works. We know what a patent is used for, we know how long it lasts—but how do you actually get one? The first step is seeing what's already out there. This is not only a critical step in the process of applying for a patent—it's an absolutely vital part of the invention process, for a number of reasons. First, you want to see if anybody else has already patented your invention-- you'd be surprised how often this happens. Second, you want to see what kind of 'room' there is for your invention—in other words, is this area of inquiry wide open, where you're likely to be able to obtain a strong, broad patent; or is it 'heavily traveled' making it unlikely that you'll be able to get patent protection of any meaningful scope or value? Finally, seeing what other people have done can often be a valuable source of ideas and inspiration which can help shape your invention.

Beware of 'invisible' inventions

Just one word of caution—when you search the patent database, you are only looking at issued patents. They may be active or expired, but they are all patents *which have issued*. You will also find patent applications which may or may not be published 18 months after submission (the inventor can elect not to have their application published). But here's the important part-- there are also going to be large numbers of patent *applications* which, as we discussed earlier, remain confidential until issued, and therefore you will not have access to them while searching—so there is always a big question mark hanging over the validity of your search. You could come up with a great search result which leads you to conclude that you have an opportunity to get a very broad patent—and on that basis you dive into the project, committing lots of time and money to develop the product and apply for a patent, only to learn a year down the road that a patent has just issued which pretty much blows your invention out of the water. This is a non-trivial consideration, particularly in view of our earlier discussion on the topic of concurrent invention. How likely do you think it is that you're the only one who has this idea for an invention? But let's not dwell on the chance of something bad happening. After all, you could walk out of your house and get hit by a bus tomorrow.

The novelty search

This process of looking at all of the issued patents to see if there's anything already out there which is 'close' to your invention is called a 'novelty search.' Remember our criteria for determining if an invention is patentable? *Novelty* is one of the key parameters, and the purpose of this search is to determine just how 'novel' your invention really is.

Again, there is no reason you can't undertake to do

a novelty search on your own, particularly if you are using it as a tool in the development of your invention. But when it comes time to prepare a patent application, you will probably want to defer to the superior skills of a patent lawyer to get a 'real' novelty search. The language and structure of the indexing and organization of patents at the PTO is arcane and convoluted and best navigated by an expert. Besides—if you have a patent attorney do a novelty search, you can also get their opinion or assessment of the merits and viability of your proposed patent. They will give you this written overview of what they have found and what the totality of the findings suggests with respect to the likelihood that you will be able to get a patent and how broadly or narrowly constrained it may be. This report is known as an 'opinion letter' and it is a critical document in deciding if, when, and how to proceed with a patent application, or even with the development of your invention. Usually a novelty search and opinion letter is not too expensive, somewhere between about $700.00 and $2000.00.

If the opinion letter concludes that it is likely that you will obtain broad patent protection and an application is deemed worthwhile, the next step is to prepare the actual patent application. This requires a full disclosure of your invention with detailed written descriptions not only of the general conceptual approach, but the details of the 'reduction to practice' and the 'preferred embodiment'—the way that you think it should be done. But don't limit yourself to only the best way—the more options you describe, the less likely someone will be able to 'work around' your patent. You will also need detailed line drawings showing how your invention works and all of the relevant components. Of course you will need your claims; but in addition, you will need to mention any 'prior art'—the patents uncovered in the novelty search—which may be relevant, and an explanation as to how your invention is a non-trivial, non-obvious improvement over this earlier work. You will also be required to demonstrate that your invention has 'utility'—meaning it is useful in a meaningful way which is an improvement over existing products—the third prong in the trident of standards which an invention must meet in order to earn a patent: novelty, utility, and non-obviousness.

Once the patent application is complete, it is filed with the PTO, and you sit back and wait. As we mentioned earlier, it usually takes the patent office at least two years to respond with a *first action*—the first communication advising what their findings are, or position is, with respect to your application. In most cases (more than 80 %), the first action will be a rejection. Don't be discouraged. Basically, the patent office rejects most applications because you have asked for too much, there is some technical problem with the way you put the application together, or you haven't been thorough enough. Ultimately, about 65% of all applications are rewarded with an issued patent.

Once you are rejected, you now have to *prosecute* your patent application. This means that you (or hopefully your patent attorney) will now have to reply to the specific objections posed by the PTO and basically prove to them that you deserve a patent.

As mentioned earlier, the longer you can maintain your 'patent pending' status, the better, so don't see a rejection as a bad thing—look on the bright side and see it as an opportunity to extend the duration of your stay in the 'no man's land' of the 'patent pending' territory.

Of course all of this costs money. Patent attorney fees, filing fees, draftsman fees—it can all add up to a non-trivial sum—most patents cost between five and ten thousand dollars, though they can run into the hundreds of thousands for complex or contested applications. That's a lot of dough to invest in an as yet unproven, unsold idea, or invention—particularly before you have earned one red cent. There's got to be a better way.

The provisional patent application

Fortunately there is a better way—the provisional patent application. This is a patent application which is filed with the PTO in much the same way that a non-provisional or "real" patent application is, with a number of important distinctions. First, at the time of this writing, the filing fee is only two hundred fifty dollars (and it's only half of this—one hundred twenty five dollars if you claim 'small entity status' which most independent inventors can). Second, the application is *not reviewed* by the PTO— it serves basically as a 'place holder' insuring that your date of invention (actually the date of submission) is documented and protected. This date is important because in the case that multiple patent applications are received by the PTO for basically the same invention, the one with the earliest submission date prevails. Third, you do not need to submit 'approved' drawings (which can be quite expensive to have produced), or claims (which require a great deal of strategic thought to prepare), which means that as long as you have worked out what your invention is and how it can be produced, you simply need to document this and you can worry about the legalistic aspects of an application later.

But the real beauty of the provisional patent application is that for one hundred and twenty five bucks you can now label your invention or product 'patent pending,' and you are essentially afforded all of the benefits and protections as those you would have had you gone to the expense and trouble of filing a full blown patent application. And you have one year from the filing date of your provisional patent application to file a non-provisional application and still maintain the filing date of your original, provisional application.

There are lots of things to know and understand about the patent application process and certain peculiarities of the provisional patent application (such as the inadvisability of submitting claims at this time) before you attempt to draft your own provisional patent application; but the task is not beyond the grasp of most individuals and the potential rewards and benefits are so great that I strongly recommend investing the time and research in becoming proficient at this skill.

The provisional patent application is an amazingly powerful, useful tool for the independent inventor, and I encourage you to get familiar with provisional patent applications and use them to your advantage.

Inventors' assistance companies

I'm not in the business of knocking anybody else's ideas, or taking the food off of anybody's table, but I have to take a moment to comment on a disturbing trend in the world of intellectual property development.

We have all seen the TV commercials for those companies that purport to help inventors market their inventions. I have also had occasion to work with a number of would-be inventors who first worked with such companies and I've come to some conclusions about these sorts of businesses.

In my opinion, based on what I have seen (and I can't say this is true of all of these companies), this is a scam—a 'racket.' Basically, these companies are trying to leverage and exploit the desire that all of us have to 'win the lottery' and make a ton of money easily, 'just like that guy who invented the Pet Rock.' As we discussed at the beginning of this book, most people have what they feel is a valuable invention or an idea for an invention, and even though they don't know what to do with it, they are secretly hopeful that they can somehow leverage it into great wealth. Most people also have no idea what a patent is or how it works, and they feel that 'if only I could get a patent on my invention, I'd be home free.' This is precisely the sort of naiveté that these companies exploit.

I had one erstwhile inventor come to me after he had been clipped by one of these companies to the tune of about fifteen thousand dollars, and proudly show me the patent they had 'helped' him obtain. The patent was poorly drafted and incredibly narrow. It was utterly worthless. I felt bad explaining this to him, but it was an important part of the process of re-educating him as to what an invention is, how it becomes a product, how you sell it, and what the role of a patent is in all of this. He realized how badly he had been duped, but there was nothing to be done about it—this company had promised him a patent, and they had delivered a patent. No one said a word about it having any value.

So don't get taken in by these scams. They are preying on our desire to make 'easy money' and let someone else do all of the hard work. Their 'kits' which are used to establish the 'date of invention' are utterly worthless—go get some real protection in the form of a provisional patent application. And their claims that they will 'submit your invention to industry' are equally bogus—as we have seen, there is a proper method and procedure for getting your invention in front of the decision makers in the carefully researched and targeted market segment in which it belongs—and this is not best accomplished by 'shot-gunning' spam or junk mail to anybody and everybody who will listen.

Step Four: Refinement

I'm beginning to sense some grumbling from the cheap seats-- "alright already—when the hell are we going to start making some money around here?" A fair question, and one which will ultimately be answered—in fact, if you subscribe to my logic, you'll find that like Captain Kirk rematerializing as he beams down to some alien world, the answer is slowly beginning to appear before your very eyes. Each piece of this puzzle gets you closer to the pot of gold at the end of the rainbow, so hang in there. Before we can make that money, we have to have something that people will buy—and in order to have something people will buy, we need to under-stand not only what constitutes a good idea, but how to translate that idea into a product that can be sold. So stick a sock in it buddy-- we're getting there.

We've already defined an 'invention,' so we might as well proceed by defining a 'product.' Since a product is a thing that a consumer will buy, and for which they will have every reasonable expectation that it will function as intended, last a long time, and not cause bodily harm or burn their house down, it is clear that a 'product' faces a much stricter set of standards than an invention. An invention simply has to be novel, practical, non-obvious, and have some utility. No one has said a thing about it being affordable, reliable, safe, durable, or any of a hundred other qualities which comprise our tacit understanding of and expectations for what a *product* is supposed to be.

So our challenge is in two parts—first, we must identify those attributes that constitute 'product-ness;' and second, we have to define the means by which we transform our 'invention' into an object which possesses these qualities and which may then, in fairness, be called a 'product.'

What expectations do you have for a product? This is a tough one, because most of our notions about such things are tacit, unspoken—sub-conscious. But if you really think about it, you can come up with some adjectives—consistent, abundant, durable, safe, good value, guaranteed, warranteed, easy to use, attractive, functional, well thought out, low maintenance, high quality, robust, well-engineered, tested, approved, competent, ergonomic, comfortable, promoted, recognized, prestigious, luxurious, environmentally responsible, and lots more. The trick here is to understand how we have accumulated this list of expectations—or more accurately, how manufacturers/marketers have succeeded in convincing us that these are attributes their products possess. To be sure, some of these qualities relate to marketing or positioning strategies—'luxurious,' 'prestigious,' etc. are intangibles which have been foisted upon us by clever advertising folks. But what of the more intrinsic values—'safe,' 'robust,' 'tested?' Where do our perceptions of these attributes come from?

We live in a mature consumer society with sophisticated expectations for the products we buy and use. In a free market, we have lots of choices competing for our discretionary income and each one attempts to distinguish itself by offering more of what we want for less money. If someone is selling widgets that have an offensive odor, and cut your fingers when you hold them, and are hard to use, they may survive or even prosper if they are the only game in town, but will pretty much go out of business when a competitor arrives on the scene with a widget that looks, works, and smells better. So there are competitive market forces at work, driving products to higher standards of quality, functionality, and value. But there's more to it than that. Living in a somewhat paternalistic and heavily regulated society, we have all sorts of government organizations looking out for our well being, legislating the risks (and some might argue the 'fun') right out of our lives. For example, the Consumer Product Safety Commission (CPSC) is charged with insuring that pretty much anything we can buy is reasonably safe—and empowered to mandate recalls if they find something that isn't. There's also the FDA, EPA, FCC, DEP, and an almost unlimited number of consumer advocacy groups (Mothers Against Widgets That Smell) happy to chime in with their two cents.

So there are free-market (competition), government mandated, and just good ol' common sense reasons why manufacturers and marketers are pushed to offer better and better products. Okay, that's the 'why,' but *how* do they make their products better?

A seasoned manufacturer establishes 'standards and procedures' manuals and practices which evolve gradually over the years to embody their understanding of the best way to solve the common problems posed in their line of business. For example, SONY demonstrates a remarkable consistency in their execution of every aspect of their consumer electronic product lines—the cases are all designed and produced with materials and methods that result in attractive, durable, functional products bearing a strong family resemblance—and they are done in a way that optimizes the capital cost/unit cost formula while minimizing development and tooling lead times, and permitting rapid introduction of new products and lines, and facilitating frequent cosmetic re-positioning. They do a great job of this, and you can bet that they have extensive procedural guides in place dictating how every aspect of every conceivable component should be handled—specifying colors and textures and radiuses and how big and what style knobs and buttons should be—pretty much every definable property of the way a thing looks, or feels, or works. This promotes uniformity in quality and appearance, and eliminates the necessity of 'reinventing the wheel' each time they undertake a new project.

Established manufacturers also understand that a little bit of time and money invested in testing before a product is released is repaid many times over through dramatically reduced returns, defects, recalls etc. There are plenty of independent testing labs out there that will put a product through the ringer, verifying that it does what it is supposed to, meets all applicable regulatory standards, and revealing any weaknesses or defects. Testing can cover a wide range of issues from environmental—temperature, humidity, water intrusion, solvent sensitivity, mechanical shock and vibration; to electronic—EMF emissions and susceptibility, electric shock sensitivity, shock hazard, etc.; to safety—choking hazard, scissor points, entrapment hazard, flammability, etc.; and durability—tensile strength of parts being pulled off (particularly important with toys for young children—i.e. how much force is required to yank off the buttons on the doll's coat which could pose a choking hazard), repetitive actuation of knobs, doors, drawers, switches, keypads, etc., drop tests, and even an extensive battery of tests designed to evaluate the shipping carton to see how well it protects the product inside.

And there are also government and private entities which certify compliance with all relevant guidelines and criteria—the most notable of which are Underwriters Laboratories (UL) in the United States and each country's independent labs such as TUV in Germany which facilitate compliance with and certification to the CE mark in the European Union. Of course, all of the testing in the world will not guarantee that your product will not experience a failure or create a hazard once it's in the hands of the consumer, but it minimizes the risk and contributes to the uniformly high quality of products in the marketplace—augmenting our perceptions of what a product 'should be.'

Industrial Design

There's another major piece of the puzzle that contributes significantly to our perception that a thing is indeed a 'product'—industrial design. This is a broad field of endeavor which is responsible for defining the look, feel, size, shape, color, and textures of a product, and specifying the materials and manufacturing processes used to create it. Industrial design is truly what transforms an invention into a product. One of the major tools used by industrial designers is 'ergonomics' or 'human factors' which is the consideration of human characteristics, capabilities, preferences, dimensions, and habits in product design—basically, designing things that work comfortably and intuitively for people; and specifying what materials and processes will be used to accomplish this. Industrial design is a crucial step in transforming an 'invention' into a 'product,' but it isn't a step that you are necessarily responsible for, or necessarily have to take to make your invention licensable—if you do, the value of your invention is definitely increased, but many companies prefer to apply their own industrial design touches to a product, so you may be wasting time, money and energy doing it yourself. Of course if you choose to manufacture and market your invention yourself, industrial design is a crucial part of the refinement process which you must undertake before you can make or sell anything.

But whether you decide to undertake a comprehensive industrial design exercise or not, you will need to be comfortable with the answers to all of the questions an industrial designer typically asks himself during the evolution of a project—how is this product going to be used; how is it going to be man-ufactured; what materials will it be made of; what are consumer expectations for this product; what should it look like; how will it be sold, packaged, displayed, stored; who is the target consumer; how could this product be abused, misused, dangerous; what message should it send to consumers; how could it be cheaper, lighter, stronger, better; what is the competition; what product is this one replacing; what product might render this one obsolete; why would a consumer want this product instead of the competition; and many others.

There are three reasons you need to go through this intensive examination of the invention—the first is that it forces you to really think about what this in-vention is, how it should work, and what its strengths and weaknesses may be, and hopefully the answers you glean will help you improve the product before it is introduced to the market; and second, this will help close that 'window of opportunity' which is created for prospective competitors if you don't do a great job on design. Third, you can be sure that a potential licensee is going to be asking all of these questions and more, and if you don't have a very good answer for each of them, they will lose confidence in you and your product and the potential deal may fizzle.

This brings up a crucial point—the value of an invention to a potential licensee is inversely proportional to the number of questions which remain unanswered. Let's take a look at what this means.

Answers equal confidence, confidence equals dollars

Only a fool would offer you money for an untested, unproven idea. If you walk into Company X and sit at their conference table, give the Chairman a steely eyed look and say in a confident, unwavering voice, "I would like to sell you my invention—it's a teleportation machine," you will probably not receive the hardy pat on the back, huge royalty advance, and congratulatory stogie you had been hoping for if, in fact, all you have brought to the table is your steely eyed look and your idea. Ideas don't mean a thing.

If, however, you can say, "I have a design for this device which I'm confident will work," you may at least get them interested enough to have one of their engineers peruse your documentation to confirm that you're a crackpot before they have security remove you from the building.

Saying, "I have a breadboard that proves my theory, though at present it only teleports squirrels," qualitatively changes the game. Suddenly, you're not a mental patient out for a stroll—you have piqued their interest as a fellow who may well be on to something.

When you can say, "I have a functioning prototype in my pocket—where would you like to go?" you have definitely crossed a line in the sand—if you can demonstrate that your invention works, you are squarely in the realm of 'let's talk about doing business together' rather than a pie-in-the-sky dreamer wasting everybody's time.

But there will still be questions—how much does it cost, how is it made, is it patented or patentable, is it based on trade secrets, do you own the rights to it, is it safe, how long will it last, how far away can it send somebody, can it bring them back? And about a million others.

Each time you answer a question by saying "I don't know," you have diminished the value of the invention. Why? Because each unanswered question represents a risk, or at the very least a development expense to the licensee. Let's say they sign a deal with you right on the spot, the very day you drag in and demonstrate your prototype. They give you a check for fifty million dollars as an advance, and promise that there's plenty more where that came from. You leave smiling, and they congratulate themselves on having just secured the single most important, and very likely, the single most lucrative invention in history. But they take a closer look and realize that your device is powered by a crystal of Kryptonite which you picked up at a Batman convention, but no more exists anywhere in the world; or they start costing out your contraption and find that each unit will cost four trillion dollars to make, and the energy required to teleport a single person is more than the annual power output of all of Canada; or they learn that in your exuberance over the early success of your invention, you published an article in the local newspaper giving precise details about how it works and how a person could build one, and you haven't gotten around to applying for a patent yet. So the invention is functionally worthless. It's a great idea, it may someday be an incredible product, but in its present state of development, it is not commercially viable. And a whole bunch of those four hundred dollar an hour lawyers we met earlier will be sending you letters politely requesting the return of the fifty million bucks.

But let's say you did your homework. You walk in,

pull your prototype out of your briefcase, teleport some insignificant assistant Vice President to the Des Moines branch office in front of everybody's eyes, then proceed to whip out a strong issued patent, fully engineered part drawings, manufacturing and QC specifications, qualified supplier and vendor lists, a fully costed Bill of Materials, and a detailed written description of the underlying science complete with the signed endorsements of several Nobel Laureate physicists attesting to both the credibility and safety of your methods, and a catchy trademarked name and advertising campaign, complete with a cute Mascot costume you sewed yourself. At this point, the only thing left to do is find a bank big enough to cash the check and let the debauchery begin. It's party time.

In most cases, it won't be so black and white. Usually, if you are smart and prepared, you will present your invention and be ready to address most of the concerns that a licensee could raise. But there will always be something, even if it's simply that the licensee has to complete the production engineering and build the tooling. You may have answered most of the pertinent questions, but you've left the door open just a hair for doubt, questions, and risk. What if, while they're in the middle of building the tooling, their competitor introduces a slight variation on the same thing which cleverly gets around the patent, does more, and costs less? Their ship is sunk before it hits the water. Is this likely? Not at all, but the point is, if you have not answered every question, if they cannot begin selling your widgets that minute, the potential for complication exists. This potential may be large or small, but rest assured—your remuneration will in large part reflect the licensee's perception of the risk remaining. The bottom line is: *the value of an invention (to a licensee) is inversely proportional to the number and scope of questions which remain unanswered.*

Three positions in the marketplace

In the example above, we talked about an invention—a teleportation machine—which was completely novel, proprietary, and unlike anything that exists. In the real world, it is extremely rare to have the luxury of such exclusivity. It is far more common to come up with a product which is an improvement over something similar. And the improvement may be in the actual utility, or it may be the price point, or it may be an intangible—it's 'cooler' or 'greener,' or endorsed by a celebrity. But rather than taking your chances that your product will find a niche in an already crowded, competitive marketplace, it would be smart to be aware of the three best positions any given product can occupy in the marketplace according to classical marketing theory which gives them a chance to succeed. As we've already discussed, the three positions are—*first, best, and cheapest*; and they are each fairly self-explanatory. Obviously, if you're not the first one to introduce a category of product, you can't be the first, so either be really novel and innovative, or take a closer look at the other two options. Being the best is always possible. Smarter design, better quality, improved functionality—it's usually not too difficult to fix the little mistakes that the competition has made and come up with something incrementally better. The problem is, there is a certain percentage of the buying public who looks for, or is willing to pay for the best (since it is almost always more expensive than the competition), but it is not a large percentage. It may be not only acceptable but downright lucrative to sell a relatively small number of widgets at a very high profit margin, but this is not a guaranteed route to success. Oftentimes, the best position to occupy is that of the 'cheapest' or least expensive—particularly if this doesn't go hand in hand with 'worst piece of crap.' If your widget pretty much looks and works just like the more costly competition, but is substantially less expensive, you will capture the market.

There is another reason why being the cheapest can be the best positioning for your invention—you get to ride along on the coattails of the 'big boys.' Think of it this way—if company A introduces their fancy schmancy version of their widget and supports it with all kinds of TV advertising and celebrity en-dorsements—which create desire in the consumer and sends him scurrying into the store—if your widget is sitting on the shelf right next to the fancy one, and yours pretty much looks, works, and feels like its more expensive competition, but is priced much lower—why wouldn't the consumer buy yours instead? So it's pretty much as though com-pany A has just paid for a bunch of advertising *for your product*.

There is a valuable lesson to be learned here for the inventor—the cheapest widget is not necessarily the one with the lowest profit margin, or the shabbiest quality—a really good reduction to practice, where every minute detail has been considered and op-timized, can do more, last longer, look better, and most importantly—cost less, than a competitive item which has not benefited from such intelligent and rigorous design scrutiny.

If you do smart design work, rigorously challenge

every detail, and price an item fairly (without trying to 'gouge' or burden the product with excessively large profit margins) you will always come out ahead.

But at the end of the day, your ultimate goal can and should be to occupy all three positions in the marketplace—first, best, and cheapest. If you are quick, smart, and reasonable you can do it, and pretty much lock up the category as your own.

Step Five: Monetization

Okay, you've come up with your idea, you've vetted it as being novel, practical and having utility, you've prototyped, refined, and protected it-- so now what?—how do you go from 'invention' to 'money making product?'

Since the ultimate goal here is to monetize your invention—to actually make money from it, you should be aware of the two fundamental options you have for doing this-- either you can manufacture and market the product yourself, or you can license it to someone else (and let them manufacture and market it). Let's take a look at what each of these options entails-- both to convey some understanding of what is involved in each and to help you choose which approach is best for you and your invention.

Understanding the rudiments of manufacturing

Think about the origins of the average product you

are familiar with in your daily life—say, a camcorder. What a wonderful product—it performs the rather remarkable task of recording audio and video reliably, economically, safely, and easily—and it costs relatively little to buy and virtually nothing to maintain—overall, an example of a great invention. And from the consumer's point of view, it's a no brainer—you go to your local neighborhood big box store or electronics discounter, pick one out that looks good and seems to do what you want it to do, and is on sale or is the lowest price, or is a brand name that you trust, and—bingo—you have a video camera. But the realities of what went into the design, engineering, manufacturing, packaging, instruction manuals, warehousing, distribution, warranty, promotion, and ultimate sale of this little bugger are almost overwhelmingly complex. Take any of the several hundred components and sub-assemblies which make up the camcorder and consider what it took to get each of these items into the assembly, and ultimately, into your hands. Let's make it even simpler and just examine a single video cassette—

the lowest common denominator ancillary item. The tape fits easily in the palm of your hand and seems like no big deal. Examine it closely and notice how many parts there are in the shell alone: the case top and bottom, the hinged tape door, the tape spools, the tensioner assembly, the recording lock slide, the felt 'wiper,' the viewing window, and a bunch of small screws, springs, and miscellaneous bits. All in all, it amounts to a few grams of plastic and steel. But think for a moment about what went into the design and manufacture of each of these parts. Every piece had to be designed and engineered to precise tolerances to function smoothly and reliably as part of a complex mechanical system (which must then interface reliably and consistently with the much, much more complex and fragile transport mechanism of the camcorder), and this design had to anticipate high volume manufacturing methods. All of the plastic parts are injection molded, which means that consideration had to be given in the design to all of the peculiarities of the injection molding process—material shrinkage had to be allowed for, draft incorporated into all sidewalls to permit extraction from the tool, the runner system and gating (the points at which molten plastic is introduced into the mold under high pressure to 'fill the mold' and make the part) configured to minimize aesthetic flaws such as 'flow marks,' and mechanical problems such as 'over-packing the mold;' ejector pins located and configured to knock the part out of the mold without deforming or damaging it; undercuts eliminated or suitable coring means designed into the mold to accommodate them; parting line locations, wall thicknesses of individual parts, and projected area of the mold cavity had to be calculated to 'balance' the mold so all parts will fill properly; the mechanical design of each part had to be optimized to be as strong as necessary while minimizing material usage and mold cycle times; wall thickness of vertical ribs reduced or restricted to less than seventy percent of the intersecting planar surface to avoid 'sink marks;' appropriate resins specified which offer adequate performance characteristics with respect to temperature range, scratch, impact,

UV, and solvent resistance, color, etc.; appropriate textures specified to be etched into the tool for an aesthetically pleasing, non-marking surface; appropriate engraving incorporated in the tool for cavity identification, production batch information, decoration, patent numbers, and product brand identification; and calculations had to be performed based on predicted sales volumes to specify the number of cavities for each component to optimize the capital cost/unit cost formula.

Once the parts are designed in this way, tooling needs to be built, tested, approved and paid for (usually tens or hundreds of thousands of dollars), and parts tested to determine safe, reliable functionality; and appropriate national or international safety or functionality certification testing scheduled, submitted to, and managed including UL Listing, CE mark, etc. Then production inventories have to be manufactured, warehoused, and paid for; assembly procedures developed and performed; QC (quality control) specs developed and implemented; records kept; and final assemblies packaged and inventoried. And all of this has to be done on a coordinated schedule so parts are available when needed, but resources are not wasted by producing or warehousing excessive quantities which will not be used any time soon. Finally, the bulk packed tape shells need to be shipped to the plant where the magnetic tape will be loaded (which is the tail end of a process of infinitely greater complexity than that described above); the assembled units undergo final QC; the tapes are loaded into cases and shrink wrapped (which involves another equally extensive set of steps including graphic design and printing); retail packaging; then inventorying, shipping to distributors or warehouses, collecting accounts payable; managing claims for defective goods and returns; and having lots of product liability insurance when you get sued, and lose, because someone inserts a tape in their nose and runs up huge medical bills as a result, all because you neglected to put a large type bold warning on the package which says, "NOT TO BE INSERTED INTO NOSE."

Next, the marketing whiz kids get in on the game and do focus groups and beta testing to come up with a catchy name and an advertising campaign that requires photo shoots and billboard and magazine ad designs and then the production of a TV commercial, and finally, massive media buys.

And let's not forget that in order to do any of this, you need to have a company, which means you have employees who get paid salaries and have benefits and retirement plans and company cars and maternity leave; and you have an office where you pay rent and utilities and taxes and insurance and legal fees, and hire a cleaning service and lease a copier, and pay someone to come in and water the plants twice a week, and your secretaries have assistants to buy coffee and paper clips and toilet paper and Christmas gifts for your best customers and suppliers.

And all of this is what needs to be done just to make the video cassette which retails for about six bucks—meaning you probably get about $3.00 for it. Now extrapolate this to cover what is needed for each and every piece of the camcorder itself; and you will start to have a sense of what is involved when you choose to be the manufacturer and/or marketer of a product. It is truly mind boggling.

And at the end of the day, if you have the good fortune to be selling a quality product at a good price, with decent profit margins, and there are no recalls or world catastrophes or boycotts which come out of left field and triple your materials costs or destroy your market, and none of your competitors suddenly introduces the latest and greatest new and improved version of the same product which does twice as much and costs half what yours does, and you don't get knocked off by cheap offshore imports—if everything goes without a hitch, you might make a net profit of about ten percent of your selling price.

Licensing 101

In contrast, let's take a look at what happens when you license a product-- you find a company that likes your product; you negotiate a deal that gives them the exclusive right to make and sell your product in exchange for them giving you a royalty on each and every one they sell—and in broad terms, a five percent royalty on net sales is a pretty reasonable industry average as far as what you can hope to negotiate-- then you go home.

Now that they have negotiated the rights to your invention, your licensee will proceed to engineer, capitalize, manufacture, advertise, market, insure, and generally bust their balls doing what manufacturers and marketers do, and ultimately, if all goes well, they will start to sell your product-- and make their ten percent net profit. Then, periodically, perhaps once each calendar quarter, they tally up all of the business they have done and cut you a check in the amount of five percent of net sales, or basically half of the net profit. This means, if you can believe it—that you have made just as much money as they have after they have assumed all of the risk, expense, aggravation, and work—and all you have to do is walk out to your mailbox and take out a royalty check, then you go back inside and read your yachting magazine because you obviously need a bigger boat.

There's another way to look at this: of the two possible routes you can follow for commercializing your product-- doing it yourself, or licensing it and letting someone else do it—one may fairly characterize them as: "the hard way," and "the easy way."

Guess which approach I prefer?

I will take a license deal over doing all of the hard work of manufacturing and marketing every time. And I do not say this idly. I have done plenty of manufacturing and marketing and it's more work than I care to do. This is not to say that there aren't reasons for and benefits to being a manufacturer—it's simply that those reasons and benefits are not compelling for me. Some people may welcome the challenges and total engagement (read: 18 hour work days) of these enterprises; and there is no disputing that you can make more money doing it this way—because the 'net profit' shared by the inventor and the manufacturer/marketer is, indeed, net of all sorts of things including your big, fat executive salary, overhead allowances, manufacturing profits, etc. And some people are really into empire building or creating a legacy, or building something to hand down to their kids. I'm not. I'd rather have tons of free time to play and enjoy my life, and if I so choose—to come up with more inventions to license to yet another bunch of hard working folks.

Can I just take a moment here to point out that the modern trend in motor yacht design towards semi-displacement hulls and twin screws not only exposes the running gear unnecessarily to damage or fouling, but is far less economical and seaworthy than a traditional full displacement hull with a single, center-line screw? What's that—you don't have time to worry about such esoteric boating nonsense?—you have to get back to work? Oh, I'm sorry—I forgot—you're a *manufacturer*. My condolences. Have fun at work. And let me know if you want to hang out on the boat some time, with the rest of my inventor friends...

While I'm sure I've beaten this point into a bloody pulp—that I find it more appealing to license a concept rather than undertaking to manufacture and market it myself—I had also intended to convey some sense of what really goes into the process, because it is important to understand these things whether you plan to do them yourself or not. A solid understanding of the demands and intricacies of manufacturing and marketing will better prepare you to deliver a product which is adequately refined and developed, and also help you understand the process and steps to commercialization, to negotiate a license agreement which is fair to the manufacturer while protecting your interests and maximizing your royalties, and to shape and direct your invention process from creative ideation through reduction to practice in order to produce products which are more attractive to the marketplace and present fewer barriers to entry insofar as they have been conceived in production friendly terms.

So those are the two choices you can make for getting your product to market—a good one or a bad one, or to put it more subtly—the right one and the wrong one (but please, don't let me influence your decision).

One final point on the manufacturing and marketing vs. licensing discussion: since it seems safe to assume that you are reading this in the United States or some other first order industrial nation, it is worth considering that we are no longer a competitive manufacturing economy for most items. The United States, for a host of cultural, socio-economic, and geo-political reasons, is a first rate innovator or source of proprietary technology and innovations; but is ill-equipped to translate this intellectual property into economically viable products. In most cases, American technology innovation (such as the DVD) is better commercially exploited/manufactured by countries which really have their hearts in the high volume/low cost manufacturing game such as China. This is an enterprise best orchestrated by huge multi-nationals—again arguing in favor of licensing them your invention and just sitting back and collecting royalty checks.

The multiplier effect

I'll leave you with one final concept to mull over—*the multiplier effect*. What exactly is the multiplier effect and why should you care about it? Imagine you work in a fast food restaurant and make seven dollars an hour. You probably dream of getting a better job where you can make twenty dollars an hour— wouldn't that be great? But the guy making twenty bucks an hour envies the patent lawyer who goes around suing all of these patent infringers and can bill his time at the astonishing rate of four hundred dollars an hour. At forty hours a week, that adds up to some serious dough. And if you can bill out eighty hours each week, you're really rolling in it. But there's one problem here—if you're working eighty hours a week, making all that money—when the hell are you going to have time to enjoy it? And what happens if you decide to take an hour or a day or a week or a month off? You stop earning money. The problem is that no matter how much money you can earn for each hour you work, you only earn money when you spend an hour working and you only have so many hours in your life—and how many of those hours do you want to spend working?

Inventing is different. If you license an invention and negotiate a royalty deal, you will earn money each time a product is sold based on your invention. This means that you do something once (come up with an invention), and then get paid for it over and over and over again. That's the multiplier effect. But there's more—the company selling these products might have five hundred salespeople out in the field, each one of them trying to hawk your wares. That means that your 'selling power' is five hundred times greater than it would be if you were one of those salesmen, getting paid by the hour, or getting paid for the fruits of your labors based on each hour you invested—instead, you earn money every single time each one of those people makes a sale. The more sales people there are, the more stores that carry your product (or catalogs or websites or infomercials)—the more money you make. And after that first bit of work to get your invention sold, you never lift a finger again. But let's say for argument's sake that you get bored counting all your money and zipping around in your yacht, and you decide to come up with another invention. It starts all over again—the multiplier effect kicks in and the checks start appearing in your mailbox for this new invention. But guess what—the royalty checks are still arriving from the first invention too. It doesn't get much better than this.

The itchy suit problem

We have thus far avoided any conversation about the 'business' aspects of inventing. It is true that the ideas, the innovation, the doodling and tinkering are all critical aspects of inventing, but to be an 'inventor' you also have to actually *sell* your inventions which means that you will be forced to deal with the many aspects of the *business* of intellectual property development. You will deal with contracts, licensing agreements, attorneys, costing spreadsheets, marketing pro-formas, and the brutal hand to hand combat of negotiating deals. And while you can invent-away sitting at your breakfast table wearing your baby blue Dr. Denton's, if you hope to actually commercialize your invention, you will be spending a great deal of time in the hallowed halls of corporate America. In those halls you will not find kindred spirits fascinated by the cleverness of your mechanisms—you will find accountants and bean counters, marketers, engineers, and generally dull, unimaginative folks whose only concern is making money from widgets and generally not giving a crap about what that widget is. And if you hope to sell your invention to these folks you have to know how to speak their language, how to play on their turf.

This doesn't mean that inventing is not a game for

clever, creative people—it means that these clever, creative people need to be equipped to function in what can be an intimidating, alien world—the corporate jungle. The most successful inventors have recognized the necessity of living with one foot in each camp and have come to embrace this ugly truth—*'inventing' is an uncomfortable, yet essential marriage between the seemingly disparate and incompatible elements of art and commerce, or creativity and business.* Neither can exist without the other, and there must be a balance between them. The better able you are to operate in both worlds; the more successful you will be as an inventor.

Markets hungry for innovation

So what industries are most receptive to taking a look at, and possibly licensing inventions from independent inventors? There are a few obvious answers, and a few not so obvious ones. The first place to look is any market segment which relies on novelty, the 'latest' gadgets, or the fickle nature of trends or fashion. Perhaps the most reliably voracious consumer of inventions is the toy industry. Why is this? Well, the toy business is in large part based on coming up with the newest, latest, greatest gizmo each and every year—particularly around Christmas time, the season where we all try to emulate Saint Santa Claus who famously said, "go ye, into the malls and big box stores, and charge ye merrily a multitude of gifts so that the meek shall be joyous this holiday season." Or something like that. In any event, the toy industry depends on having something new, exciting, and irresistible each holiday season, and they are wide open to the possibility that the next big one—the next Rubik's Cube, or Cabbage Patch doll, or Beanie Baby will come to them from an outside inventor. Most toy companies have 'product idea submission forms' that protect their interests as well as those of the inventor, and generally try to make it as easy and comfortable as possible for all parties to maintain an open discourse about new ideas.

This same attitude is also found in other market segments where the 'latest and greatest' is in high demand. Companies that sell products on TV—particularly infomercials, are always on the prowl for the 'next big thing.' This is also true in the automobile industry, or any other industry where 'model years' and regularly scheduled new product introductions require that there be some new feature or bells and whistles that distinguish this year's offerings from the hopelessly obsolete old junk they were hawking last year. The automobile industry can sometimes be a tough sell for a number of reasons—they are very large corporate monoliths with convoluted and difficult to navigate channels of communication and onerous requirements for testing and validation, and tremendous price pressure, but the point (which may be readily applied to other markets) is that they *need* new ideas on a regular basis.

Another place to look for receptive licensees for your invention is in a commodity marketplace. This means any business where there are a whole bunch of people selling pretty much the same product, and there is no real point of difference between competitors' products. In such businesses, it is a game of fractions of a penny, where each manufacturer is scrambling to reduce costs and cut profit margins so they can sell their product at the lowest price point (which is the only thing the consumer cares about when they see no difference between product offerings) yet still make enough money to keep the doors open and the lights on. It is a brutal, ugly business environment and it can make people very cranky. Why on earth would you want to talk to these sullen bastards? Because if you can offer them the Holy Grail of the commodity product manufacturer—*a proprietary advantage*—you can liberate them from the rat race, where everybody is fighting over scraps, and elevate them to the world of unchallenged, fat profit margins.

What is a 'proprietary advantage?' The term 'proprietary' basically means something that is owned and/or controlled by a single entity. It is the opposite of a commodity, which is something in the 'public domain' or freely available to anyone who wants to use it. A proprietary advantage is afforded by an invention or a product feature which only one company has, which has clearly discernable benefits and advantages for the consumer, and which distinguishes this company's offerings from those of all of his competitors. To a commodity product manufacturer, a proprietary advantage is a license to print money.

An example is the pencil business. Lots of companies make pencils. Do you have a favorite brand of pencil, or look for special features? If you're like me, on the rare occasion that you actually go to a store to buy a pencil, you make sure it's yellow, it has an eraser on top, and a little number '2' printed on the side. Other than that, I try to buy the package which has the most pencils in it for the lowest price. Welcome to the hell that pencil manufacturers everywhere wake up to every day. But what if one pencil manufacturer had a proprietary advantage—some kind of feature that sets their pencils apart from everybody else's—let's say, their pencil lead stops writing when it senses that it has strayed outside of those infamous little circles that we've all colored-in countless times while filling out machine readable forms or answer sheets on standardized tests. This is something that really improves the utility of the product—it offers a clearly recognizable benefit to the consumer, and if it only costs a little bit more than a plain vanilla pencil, why wouldn't everybody buy one? Obviously, that's just a fictional example, but the point should be clear—if you can offer a manufacturer who is mired in the commodity business a proprietary breath of fresh air—a point of differentiation for his products—which is novel, practical, has utility, and can belong exclusively to him, you may find yourself getting both a large check and a very enthusiastic kiss on the lips from a sweaty, hairy, out of shape man with a lot of pencils in his pocket— your new business partner.

How do you identify companies to approach with your invention?

Once you have your invention ready to go, you

need to figure out where it's going *to*. Who are you going to approach with your idea? It's generally not too difficult to narrow down the list to a particular market segment—for example, if you've invented the pencil we discussed above, you're probably not going to be calling Ford, or Godiva, or Timex. You'll be looking in the direction of the companies who are already in the business of making writing instruments generally, or pencils specifically. So let's say you've decided to start by approaching a pencil company. Great. How do you pick which one to go to out of the dozens that exist? Well, you have to consider a number of factors. First of all, you want a company which is big enough, or dominates the segment enough to do a good job getting your invention out there. Second, you want a company in good financial health, so they likely have the resources to commit to developing and marketing a new item. And third, you want a company with a reputation, or at least a proclivity for trying new things, taking chances, being innovators. And how do you know which companies meet these criteria? Easy—it's called the internet. It is absolutely astonishing what you can learn by doing a few well directed searches on Google over the course of an hour or so. And once you have identified the likely suspects, make a few phone calls. We'll talk more later about who you try to speak with and what you say to them, but let's assume for the time being you actually get an intelligent human being on the phone and you chat with them in broad terms, without disclosing anything confidential, about what you've come up with and what their needs and interests may be. This is oftentimes the single most informative, valuable education you can get as far as the specifics of the market you are trying to break into. Remember— most inventors don't specialize in any particular field; and I know that for me personally, it is very often true that each project I undertake will be my very first foray into a given industry. For that reason, I may not know a thing about how this industry thinks or works, or the history of what has been attempted. I probably won't know the lingo they use. I may think I've come up with the greatest idea for a coffee pot ever, only to learn anecdotally in the first conversation I have with someone who's actually in the business that the big joke in the industry is about how some schmuck came up with an idea for a coffee pot that blew up and killed someone about fifteen years ago, and nobody has ever dared present a similar idea. Coincidentally, it's exactly the invention I called to pitch. Ooops. Back to the drawing board.

The point is, you can and will learn so much in the course of your first exchange with a potential licensee that I generally don't select the company I really want to do business with as my first contact. I usually go after a second or third choice knowing that in the first cold call I probably won't have the jargon down, I won't know what the industry trends are, I won't know what the 'Holy Grail' of the industry is—basically, I'll be (and sound like) a naïve jackass, but I will soak up all of the information so on my next call I'll sound like someone who's been immersed in the industry for years. Sometimes saving the best, not for last, but for second or third can be a smart strategy.

There are other factors to consider when researching what companies you want to approach with your invention. Sometimes the biggest player is not the best. There are a couple of reasons why this may be so. First, they may be quite content being number one, making lots of money, and dominating the market. Frequently, it is the number two player who is hungrier and more aggressive, and therefore more likely to be on the lookout for that competitive advantage. Perhaps the very invention you've come up with is precisely what they want, need, and dream of to slip them into the lead. Second, the biggest players in a given segment may have too much invested in the 'old way' of doing things, so they may have a strong disincentive to switch to your new way. Sometimes the momentum of substantial capital investment, infrastructure, or just plain habit can be a formidable obstacle to overcome, and a newer player in the game with less invested or a more aggressive growth strategy may be an easier sell.

Surprisingly, you may find that you don't want to pitch your invention to a company which is in the pencil business at all. You may learn that all pencil manufacturers are mired in the primitive manufacturing and marketing techniques of the late nineteenth century and have grave suspicions about technology and mistrust new ideas. It could be that they are so married to doing things the way they've always been done that they simply are not open to the possibility of a new idea—even if it's an idea which could completely transform their business if they adopt it, or put them out of business if they don't. In such a circumstance, you may find that you are well advised to speak with a potential competitor who is swimming at the fringes of the pencil industry—a company making products which are sold through the same distribution channels, or a company which makes standardized 'fill in the dot' forms, which would be a natural partner for your invention. It could be a company which wants to, or would be well advised to integrate their product line vertically, or expand laterally, and end up in the pencil business even if they aren't there at the moment. Or it could be a company which has never even looked at a pencil before, let alone thought of manufacturing one, but is keen on hot new products and sees an opportunity in yours. The point is this— keep an open mind about the breadth of possibilities in the companies you can, should, and do approach as prospective licensees.

This is all great in theory, but in reality, you will find that a company which seems to be the ideal candidate on paper may not work out at all, for a number of reasons. As mentioned earlier, some companies are more receptive than others to outside submissions. Obviously, a company bristling with defenses against independent inventors is not going to be as easy or desirable a target as one that welcomes you with open arms. Sometimes the decision to approach one company over another is based on something as simple as geographic proximity. If two companies are potential targets and one of them is located across the country from you, while the other one is down the block—all other things being equal, it certainly makes sense to try to work with your neighbor before you hop on a plane.

And finally, besides geographic accessibility, there are other types of access to consider. It is always better to go to a company where you have some kind of 'in' such as a friend or relative who works there or knows someone who works there or you went to school with their kid, or your kids play soccer together. Any kind of 'less than arm's length' relationship can be an enormous advantage—not so much in terms of improving the odds of signing a deal, but in gaining access, making it through the protective phalanx of automated voicemail systems, overly protective secretaries and assistants, and busy executive schedules and actually getting to speak to a real human being who is authorized and qualified to speak with you about your invention. Once you get out there and start trying to contact prospective licensees, you will find that access is everything.

So you've identified the company you'd like to pitch your invention to—great. Who do you talk to and what do you say to them? If the company is fairly small, the best person to speak with is the owner, especially if that person is also the founder. There are two reasons for this: first, in a small company, it is likely that every decision, particularly those about spending money or changing the product line, will be handled by the owner/founder, so you're pretty much wasting your time going anywhere else. The second and more important reason is that the kind of person who can start and operate a company generally has a very different nature, personality, and mindset than the kind of person who applies for a job to work there. What I mean by this is that it takes real vision, a true entrepreneurial spirit to start a company, and that's exactly the kind of risk-taking attitude and forward looking vision that's needed to both see the value in an invention and invest the time, money, and effort to bring it to market.

If you can't reach the founder/owner, and you are forced to speak with an underling, bear in mind that this person very likely lacks the drive, charisma, intelligence and foresight of the person who put this company on the map, and you're going to have to approach them in a fundamentally different way. This is particularly true of 'second generation' employees—where the founder/owner's son or daughter is in charge. Almost without exception the offspring of the risk-taker who made it all happen are of a much more conventional constitution, and aren't capable of the same visionary actions as the old man.

If the company you'd like to approach is medium to large size, it is very likely that not only will it be impossible to gain access to the founder/owner (or they may have died many generations ago), but they may not be involved in the daily operations of the company, even in something as crucial and fundamental as licensing new products. So you will be forced to seek out the appropriate employee. If the company is 'inventor friendly' meaning they actively solicit, or at least tolerate outside inventions, there may very well be an employee whose job title is something like 'outside submissions coordinator' or 'inventor liaison.'

It's more likely that your target company will not have a dedicated outside invention coordinator, so you will need to get to the person responsible for new product development. How do you find them? The first way is doing research. I frequently Google the company name along with keyword phrases like "new products" or "product development" or "vice president product development" in the hopes of finding some blurb in an industry magazine that mentions so and so's promotion to this position, or an award they just got for doing something—and this information can be amazingly valuable in helping to identify the person you want to speak with. If this fails, ask the receptionist—the person who answers the phone at the company switchboard. Just say something like, "would you please tell me who

I can speak to about an invention I'd like to share with your company?" or "can you tell me who is responsible for new product development at your company?" Again, if it's a company which regularly considers outside submissions, the operator will probably know to whom she should direct your call.

If there is no person at the company who obviously bears the responsibility for reviewing outside submissions, try asking for the Director of Marketing. While marketing couldn't have less to do with the technical evaluation of a potential submission, it has everything to do with understanding what the company's customers are looking for. Think about it— even though it is likely that the marketing people are completely non-technical and non-creative, they may well be your strongest ally in getting your invention the attention it needs within the company to secure a licensing deal. Imagine the scene in the office as the marketing guy you just spoke with puts your call on hold and rushes into the president's office and says, "I've got a guy on the phone who says he can make a pencil that won't draw outside the lines! We could sell the bejeezus out of that!"

The one group of people you *don't* want to talk to is the engineering or technical staff. Engineers are notorious for lacking the business savvy or foresight to see the value in an invention, and nowhere else is the NIH syndrome more powerfully embedded. What is "NIH" syndrome? "Not Invented Here"—or "CYA" (Cover Your Ass) where there is a great deal of resistance or even overt hostility towards any-thing new which didn't originate from within the company, based on the mistaken assumption that anything good which employees failed to come up with on their own somehow threatens their jobs or credibility. You will not find love, compassion, or as-sistance forthcoming from a bunch of unimagina-tive, angry engineers who see you as a threat, or at the very least believe you to be making them look bad. The best they can hope for is that you'll simply disappear, so anything they can do to facilitate that is something they'll happily undertake.

There is a very important aspect of the 'corporate mentality' or 'corporate culture' that you need to understand before picking up the phone. Except for the founder/owner, everybody else you might speak to is an employee. An employee is a very different kind of creature than an entrepreneur. The mindset of a person who wants to work for somebody else, who seeks the security of a job rather than the risk, benefits, and adventure of creating their own enterprise, is something that is worth understanding because it is this mindset rather than any obstacles presented intrinsically by your invention which will be the biggest hurdle you have to clear. And it is not only the mindset of the employee, but the attitude of the corporation which you will have to overcome— most companies reward employees who maintain the status quo.

This seems somewhat counter-intuitive—don't companies want their employees to make big, exciting changes and advance the company's business by giant leaps? Well, in theory yes, but here's what really happens—if an employee does something really big, really great, they may get a nice commendation and a little blurb in the company newsletter. But if they do something really bad—make a really big mistake—which you can only do if you take a really big chance—then they get fired. If, however, the employee keeps a low profile—doesn't take any chances, doesn't make any big moves, they just maintain the status quo—they will be thought of as a 'model employee' and will continue to advance up the corporate ladder with annual reviews and raises. So the corporate culture does not *explicitly* discourage risk-taking, it does so tacitly, in a much more powerful, compelling way.

So what's the bottom line here? Employees are not rewarded for taking risks—and you, my inventor friend, are a risk.

This is why, when trying to reach an employee at a company, you have to be very careful about what you will say and how you will say it. Remember, the person on the other end of the line is going to be busy, harried, and worried about taking chances that could lose him his job. He doesn't need the aggravation that you are bringing. Even if he somehow accidentally or begrudgingly picks up the phone and speaks to you, you have to be aware of the fact that of all the things he's worried about in dealing with a potential 'big mistake,' the very first one is his concern that he will somehow compromise himself and the company by accidentally or inadvertently accepting a confidential disclosure from you, which now exposes the company to all sorts of unpleasant legal liabilities. For many reasons, there is a strong disincentive for any employee to talk to you. Understand this before you open your mouth.

So when you do open your mouth, you had better say something right away, which is going to allay the fears of the person you are speaking to. Remember that the best way to win someone over is to address *their* concerns, not yours. You are calling because you have come up with a great invention and you want someone to spend all the money and assume all of the risk and bring your invention to market so you can make a shitload of money and never have to work again. A careful explanation of this is not going to win you any friends or advance your cause. Think about what the person on the phone wants, needs, and is terrified of—and do your best to couch your presentation in terms which address these concerns. You won't get anywhere close to getting what *you* want until you give this person what *they* want.

You can start off by saying something like, "Hi, my name is Blah Blah (though I'd recommend that you use your real name, as 'blah blah' can be off-putting), and I'm a professional inventor." Sometimes the invocation of a term like 'professional' can be very soothing to the terrified soul on the other end of the line. After all, they too are a professional so you already have something in common. Also, a professional it would seem would know how to go about doing things in a way that isn't going to make a big mess and put this guy's ass in a sling.

"I've done some research and identified your company as the best positioned to benefit from some proprietary technology I've developed which offers consumers an enormous perceived advantage with a nominal incremental manufacturing cost, and which would really set your company's products apart in a crowded commodity marketplace."

I realize this sounds complicated, like I just crammed ten pounds of crap into a five pound sack, but this is the key to the whole thing. Not only is there a huge amount of business type information contained in this sentence, there is enough psychology packed in here to teach a whole semester of Psych 101. Let's go through it piece by piece.

By starting out with the phrase "I've done some research and identified your company..." you are communicating that not only have you done your homework and looked into the matter (so you are now an educated or qualified observer), but you have selected this guy's company as being the special one, the right one for whatever it is you have. People like to be singled out for praise—to have their 'special-ness' recognized and acknowledged and this innate desire can even be stretched to include the propri-etary feelings many people have for the company which employs them.

"… benefit from proprietary technology…" is an-other potent tidbit which tells your erstwhile partner a couple of very important things—first, something good, not bad, will come of all this, and second, what you bring to the table is proprietary which means it is going to help one company and only one company and if it isn't his, it may well be the com-petition's, which would be bad—so not only is this an opportunity for something good to happen for his company, it is equally an opportunity to prevent something bad from happening; or it is possibly a subtle veiled threat—if you don't work with me, I'm going to your competition.

Next, you give him a few key phrases that convince

him you not only know what the invention game is all about but you understand what his company, and by implication he needs out of all of this— "offers consumers enormous perceived benefit with a nominal incremental manufacturing cost." This demonstrates that you understand that ultimately it's all about the consumer—not because anybody cares about the consumer, but because it's the consumer who drives sales, who gives you their money and if you don't understand that you have to entice the consumer, you don't understand anything. Also, it is implicit in the part about "nominal incremental manufacturing cost" that you not only have a handle on how things are made and what the costs of various manufacturing methods are, but you have some sense of how much it costs them to make their current product, how much more it will cost to make yours, and more importantly, you recognize that substantial cost increases are a bad thing.

And the zinger is "which could really set your company's products apart in a crowded commodity marketplace." This is like *giving* candy to a baby—you have just handed him the Holy Grail of the commodity manufacturer—a proprietary advantage which will distinguish his products from those of his competition so he can rise above the fray, stop fighting over fractions of a cent, and start making a healthy profit. You are really speaking this guy's language. And that's the key.

If you had instead called up and blurted out, "I'm a really smart inventor and I want you to buy my invention so we can both make a lot of money!" You wouldn't have communicated anything fundamentally different—basically you were saying exactly the same thing as you said the first time; but your message has been stripped of the subtleties and nuances which convey your awareness of and sensitivity to all of those things that the employee and company are scared of and worry about. With your more refined version, you have turned the tables so you are not seen as the bad guy or a potential mistake—instead you come across as one of them, a good guy, a knight on a white horse come to save the day.

With any luck, if you've delivered that opening salvo convincingly, you should be able to elicit a response somewhat along the lines of, "that sounds great, we'd love to hear more." Should you be so lucky, you want to again reinforce your sensitivity to the company's concerns and say something like, "I understand your concerns about receiving confidential submissions—do you have some sort of standard submission form or Confidential Disclosure Agreement you'd like to use, or shall I send you a copy of the agreement I've always used?" Note how the inclusion of the little word 'always' subtly implies that you are a seasoned and experienced inventor, reinforcing the perception that you are a good thing rather than a disaster waiting to happen.

And this is how it begins. Oftentimes the biggest hurdle is getting your foot in the door. Once you're able to get your invention in front of the decision makers, it will be the merits of the product that decide its fate—but until then, the chances for success hinge almost entirely on your ability to verbally articulate and convey your experience with, sensitivity to, and competence in addressing the wants, needs, and concerns of the company.

Why a company may not want your great invention

Even if you manage to bob and weave your way through the convoluted corporate defenses, and find yourself in the inner sanctum with the opportunity to pitch your invention to the people who are in a position to make something happen—you may find that your brilliant idea falls on deaf ears. How could this be?

There are lots and lots of reasons why a company chooses to pass on an idea rather than snatch it up and run with it. Remember NIH Syndrome? Remember our little chat about corporate culture rewarding those who 'don't rock the boat' rather than those who take chances? These are powerful obstacles to overcome, but there are more.

Bringing a new product to market—taking it from invention to the store shelf, is an incredibly costly enterprise in terms of time, money, energy and resources. Every company has only a limited quantity of each of these, and it may be a corporate decision that the commercialization of your invention, even your great invention, is simply too much of a drain on capital to make sense. Hasn't this happened to you in your own personal life? Haven't there been times when you saw something you really, really wanted to buy but just couldn't because you would have been spending your rent money or your grocery money or the money you had set aside to buy that pony for your niece? It may even have been the keyboard you absolutely *needed* in order to get your garage band out of the garage and well on its way to superstardom, but you just couldn't make it happen. Corporations are no different than you— they have to make pragmatic decisions about how to allocate their finite resources. This may seem stupid or shortsighted or unfair, but it is none of these—it is a simple reality of the marketplace; and it should serve to underscore the importance of identifying in your research companies that not only have the resources to commercialize your invention, but have demonstrated the corporate will to do so in the past.

Size matters

Another reason a company may pass on your invention is because it is not 'big enough' for them. It could be that your invention will easily be a ten million dollar a year business. But if you are a monstrously large corporation, a ten million dollar a year business is more of an accounting inconvenience than an opportunity of a lifetime. It is quite common for large companies to have a minimum threshold annual dollar volume below which they will not consider venturing. The logic for this is surprisingly fairly solid. It may seem crazy to us for someone to pass on a ten million dollar business, but try to see it from the company's perspective—it takes pretty much the same amount of money, the same number of employees, and the same amount of time to launch any given new product (this is, of course, a gross generalization, but bear with me for the sake of the argument)—so why invest these resources in a ten million dollar business when you could invest them in a fifty million dollar business? Also, keeping track of a whole bunch of small businesses is more of a hassle than tracking a smaller number of mid- to large size businesses.

There is a further variation on this 'too small' theme—some companies are not interested in a 'product,' they are only interested in 'product lines.' For example, in the case of our pencil which won't write outside of the lines, a large company which is not already in the pencil business probably wouldn't license the invention because it would be an oddball in an otherwise closely related family of products or businesses. If, however, you could give them a whole 'line' of products and put them into a new business, this might be a much more attractive proposition. There are a number of reasons for this—first, it is logistically difficult for a company to manage a stand alone, oddball product. If they are not already in the office supply business (let's say they sell sporting goods), this pencil invention doesn't fit in anywhere in their corporate structure or mentality. And in practical terms—if they don't have any contacts with the buyers of office equipment, if they have no existing customers in this segment, then they are pretty much 'fish out of water' in their efforts to penetrate this marketplace. If, however, you approached them not with a *single* 'magic' pencil, but with an *entire line* of 'magic' writing implements, or a line of pencils and another of erasers, and a third of special pads or paper, there may now be enough of a 'critical mass' of products to constitute a 'product line' and justify the foray into the category.

The second reason your invention may be 'too small' is that companies are developing internally, or receiving outside submissions for new products on a continual basis. It is possible that even though your idea is a good one, and will very likely do respectable business, that there is another invention which comes along at the same time which is a little bit (or a lot) better, and which will probably do more business. In this instance, there is nothing wrong with your invention, there's just something more 'right' about somebody else's. This happens from time to time; and when it does, you generally have two choices—start looking for another company to license to, or put this invention in the closet and move on to the next big idea.

Are you compatible?

The final thing you need to think about is that an invention, and the product it will ultimately become, may simply not be a good fit for the company you are targeting. It may seem to fit in their current product line; but what you don't realize is they have made a corporate strategy decision to steer their product lines away from the current mix; or they have decided to focus future growth on a new category which they have identified as being more profitable, or having greater potential. Or it could, quite by chance, look a little too much like a product they tried a few years back which resulted in legendary losses or lawsuits.

Ultimately, they may just not 'get it.' I have seen this happen countless times—I will approach a company with an invention that I personally think is truly brilliant—an opportunity to completely transform their business, and the genius sitting across the desk with the blank stare and mouth hanging open with flies freely buzzing in and out will in a slow, monotone voice say, "what... do... you...mean?" At which point it is generally best to gather up the dog and pony show, shake his hand and thank him for his time, and silently utter a prayer of gratitude that both of your parents had 32 chromosomes. Sometimes it just isn't meant to be. This doesn't mean that your invention isn't great, or you're not a genius—it just means that there is a massive conspiracy in place designed to drive you insane and prevent you from succeeding. Or, it could mean that you haven't knocked on the right door yet. Keep knocking, eventually that door will open and it will make all of the bullshit worthwhile.

Unfortunately, at this point I need to make you aware of one small fly in the ointment—a market-place reality which can sometimes make the work of an independent inventor a lot harder. Sometimes the very company that wants and needs precisely the invention you have just come up with—won't look at it. Why the hell not?

It's a curious thing—the very lifeblood of our economy, the survival and economic well-being of individual companies, depends on the steady intro-duction of new products and innovative new ideas, but there is a tremendous reluctance on their part to look at what are termed 'outside submissions.' There are two principle reasons for this. The first is one of the darker aspects of human nature, stem-ming from pride, jealousy, and insecurity—it is (as we've already discussed), "Not Invented Here (or NIH) Syndrome." Unfortunately, many people who are in a position to make something happen with your invention don't want to know about it because it somehow makes them feel threatened or dumb or inadequate if *you* thought it up instead of *them*. Or they feel that it can't be any good because you're an outsider and how could you possibly know anything about their business or their products or their customers' wants and needs? Or they may feel as though they're paying their own employees a whole lotta money, and why the hell aren't they coming up with these ideas? Finally, they may feel as though it is cheaper for them to use only internally generated ideas, because then they don't have to pay any royalties (based on the assumption that ideas developed by employees are the property of the company automatically). Of course, these are all tragically flawed rationalizations, but human nature is a strange beast, and you might as well know what you're up against.

The second reason many companies don't want to

consider outside submissions is a much more pragmatic one—they don't want to get sued. Living as we do in such a litigious society, it is not only understandable, but probably a good survival strategy to do whatever you can to reduce the likelihood that someone is going to sue you. Unfortunately, the history (and law) books are full of cases where individual 'inventors' sued big companies claiming that their idea had been stolen—and in the majority of these cases, the individual prevailed. This has understandably left a very bad taste in the mouth of many corporations, and made them rather gun shy, or reluctant to consider outside submissions.

How do these situations arise in the first place? As we discussed earlier, since we all live in a world where we share a common understanding and background and where our ultra efficient communications and media channels bring pretty much the same news to all of us more or less at the same time, and these factors contribute to simultaneous independent 'inventions,' one can see how it is not only possible, but *likely* that a large company with a great deal of resources focused on the continuing evolution, improvement and expansion of their product lines may very well be working on, or have at the very least considered the exact same thing you just came up with and would like to present to them. If they take a look at your invention and say, "that's a great idea-- in fact, it's so great, we've already been working on it and we're planning on introducing a new product based on this invention next spring," what is the first thought that's going to pop into your head? "Those bastards are stealing my idea!" It's a perfectly natural and reasonable conclusion to come to. And it may be accurate. Or it may not. The problem is that the courts have been asked many times to decide the merits of such cases and in the majority of them, they have decided in favor of the little guy. Want a little hint as to why this happens? Think about a jury trial where the 'jury of your peers' has to decide whether little ol' you is picking on the big, bad, deep pockets corporation, or vice versa. How many of those peers are Chairmen of corporations sympathetic to the plight of the big boys, and how many of them are Average Joes, fully convinced of the existence of myriad conspiracies against the little guy in both the corporate and government sectors? Towards which party are their sympathies and allegiances likely to lean? Precisely. So, as a practical matter of survival, it has just become easier for large corporations to institute 'no outside submissions' policies.

But there is a better way for corporations to resolve this issue than burying their collective heads in the sand and refusing to look at anything—a smarter solution which is a compromise between the desire to see what exciting new things are going on out there, and the necessity of covering one's ass. Whether it is called a Confidential Disclosure Agreement, or a Submission Policy, the use of a legally binding document which unambiguously defines the terms under which you the inventor are willing to disclose, and the company is willing to review, your invention, is a powerful tool for defining and controlling the terms of submission of an invention and avoiding the aforementioned problems.

Generally speaking, such an agreement will address the following issues:

1. Parties to the agreement. This defines who is who and what each is permitted or entitled to do.

2. Purpose of the agreement. This states that you, the inventor, wish to submit to the company for consideration an invention you have come up with, and that the company is willing, under clearly defined terms, to review your submission.

3. Terms of the submission. This is the most important part of the agreement. It specifies precisely the terms under which you are submitting, and the company is agreeing to review your invention. Generally, it includes language that states that the fact of your submitting, and the fact of the company's agreeing to review, does not obligate either of you to enter into a business relationship with the other. Then, it will

clearly state that the company will not share your idea with anybody outside of its own employees or those necessary to evaluate its merits, but will in any event make every effort to protect the confidential nature of your invention, and will only disclose it to others under very limited precisely defined circumstances. And finally, there is language which states that the company may not use your invention unless you enter into a mutually agreeable business relationship, except under the following conditions:

a.   if they have already come up with the same idea internally as documented by written records (which eliminates the 'trust' issue);

b.   if this invention was or is brought to them by an independent third party with no obligations of confidentiality under the controlling agreement (in other words—if they can show that an unrelated third party inventor showed them the same thing they are under no obligation to work with you);

c.   or, if they can show that the invention is already known in the public domain or though other non-confidential, non-proprietary sources.

4.   Finally, there will be a term of the agreement which states that the company will be obligated by all of the stipulations of the contract (including maintaining confidentiality and agreeing not to use the invention without your permission or entering into a business relationship with you) for a set period of time.

Here's a copy of the Confidential Disclosure Agreement that I have used for over twenty years. Most companies who are willing to enter into this kind of relationship find this agreement to be fair and acceptable.

CONFIDENTIAL DISCLOSURE AGREEMENT

Date

Dear   ,

You have requested that I provide you with certain information described in Appendix A hereto (the "Confidential Information") for the purpose of evaluation in connection with a possible business arrangement with me. In consideration of my disclosure of the Confidential Information, you hereby agree:

1.   The Confidential Information will be received by you for the sole purpose of evaluation as outlined in the first paragraph of this letter, and you will not use it for any other purpose.

2.   The Confidential Information will not be disclosed to others, or reduced to writing in the form of drawings or otherwise, or reproduced by you for a period of three (3) years from the date of this letter without specific authorization in writing from me, except to the extent required to be disclosed to your officers or to others necessarily involved in your evaluation if they agree in writing to be bound by the terms of this letter. However, no obligation or restriction shall be imposed on you with respect to any of the Confidential Information which:

A.   was known to you prior to the date of this letter as evidenced by written records;

B.   was publicly known prior to the date of this letter, or which became publicly known thereafter, through no act or failure of yours; or which became known to you through a third party who is free of obligation not to disclose such Confidential Information.

C.   is required to be disclosed by judicial or governmental action.

3.   You will take all reasonable steps to insure that the obligations and restrictions imposed on you by this letter are observed by your officers, partners, agents, and employees.

4.   If after your evaluation of the Confidential Information, you desire to enter into further business arrangements in connection with my invention, such arrangements with me will be separately negotiated. Nothing herein grants you any rights to my invention or obliges me to sell, grant or license this invention to you or to enter into any business arrangement with you.

5.   You will return the Confidential Information and all copies thereof made by you, at any time we so request. Your agreements in paragraphs 1, 2, and 3 will survive return of the Confidential Information.

6.   The Confidential Information will be received by you in accordance with the terms of this letter regardless of any contrary or inconsistent conditions otherwise expressed.

If you are in agreement with the foregoing, please so indicate by executing below and returning one copy to me.

Very truly yours,

(Inventor Name)

Agreed:

For   ,

By: _____

Date: _____

APPENDIX A

Description of Technical Information/Invention

"new product concepts"

If a company agrees to sign a Confidential Disclosure Agreement such as this, consider yourself to be very fortunate. It is now easy to share your inventions with them and feel that you are protected both from them stealing anything from you and any compromise of the confidentiality of your ideas-- in case they aren't interested and you move on to another prospect.

Many companies, however, will insist on a very different kind of Submission Agreement. Their agreements explicitly state that they will not agree to accept or hold any disclosures in confidence, and they will not honor any rights you as an inventor may have except those recognized and granted under United States Patent and Copyright law. Basically they are saying—'don't show us anything you don't want us to steal or blab about to everyone we know, unless you have a patent to protect yourself.' This is a much trickier situation to deal with. As we discussed earlier when we talked about patents, it is not practical to apply for a patent or wait for a patent to issue for every idea you have, particularly if you are reasonably prolific. So in these situations you may have to make a judgment call. Obviously, the first thing to do is to try and find another company to talk to and see if they aren't willing to enter into a more reasonable and balanced disclosure relationship—but if these are the guys you want or need to talk to, particularly if you've struck out everywhere else, or there's nowhere else to go, it might just be worth taking the chance.

There are a few things to bear in mind in these situations. First, no company in their right mind is going to flagrantly steal an idea from you, even if you have signed such an agreement. Again, legal history tells us that such actions are heavily punished in the courts. Second, odds are that if your idea really has merit, the company will make every effort to work out an equitable deal with you in exchange for the rights to your invention. And finally, sometimes it comes down to rolling the dice and saying, 'hey, I'd rather take a chance that something may happen here, even if there is a risk that my invention may be stolen, than keep my idea safely locked away in the vault where it is guaranteed both never to be stolen and never to be licensed.'

What's it worth?

So let's say you've come up with an invention (or better yet, a whole bunch of inventions) that meets our criteria of utility, novelty, and practicality. How do we know (or guess) what each of them is worth—and by implication, which of them is most promising or most worth pursing? The simple answer is—we can't. You could come up with an idea that I think is utterly preposterous and wouldn't give you two cents for, then make $100 million on it overnight. As P T Barnum said, "No one ever lost money underestimating the taste of the American public." So there are no absolutes in estimating the value of an invention; but we can take a stab at it by looking at just how novel and just how much utility a given invention has—while its 'practicality' or ability to be produced as an economical, durable, reliable, functional product is presumed to be a given—if the product can't be made for a reasonable cost, doesn't work, or falls apart, it will never succeed.

Let's look at an example. If factories everywhere are churning out blue door stops and I come up with the brilliant idea of making a red one; that's probably a legitimate invention—it can be made, it's novel (albeit very slightly) and it has some utility (a trivial aesthetic distinction over the existing competition). But the financial value of this invention is pretty marginal—the only thing novel about it is a really minor distinction over the existing competitive products and that distinction has nothing to do with its basic utility (holding a door open). I'm probably not going to retire or set the world on fire with this one.

If, however, everybody in the world relies on planes, trains and automobiles to travel and I come up with a safe, reliable, economical teleportation device, which can instantly transport a person to any location in the world, it is safe to say that I will not be waiting for the day old donuts to go on sale at my local grocery store before indulging my sweet tooth any longer—by which I mean—I'll be rich as hell. And the difference between my teleporter and my blue door stop? It is the *degree* of novelty and utility.

Unfortunately, history is rife with examples of inventions which were truly revolutionary—they represented enormous leaps forward in novelty and utility—which never went anywhere. In some cases, they were too far ahead of their time, in some cases it was a confluence of unfortunate events, or poor business sense, or just plain inexplicable bad luck.

So again, it is impossible to forecast the market value, or the ultimate financial return of an invention, but one can make rough estimates based on the intrinsic degrees of novelty and utility.

Serial vs. parallel submissions

Just a quick note about how you present your invention to the marketplace. We have talked about the very high attrition rate of inventions—how you will probably have to talk to a whole bunch of companies before you finally find one which 'takes the bait.' So it may be tempting to adopt a 'shotgun' approach in your efforts to find a home for your invention—submitting it to a lot of companies simultaneously in the hopes that at least one of them will be interested. One could certainly argue the merits of such an approach, but I have found that a 'serial' (one at a time) approach works much better than the 'parallel' (all at once, or 'shotgun') approach for a number of reasons. First, can you imagine how sticky a situation gets if more than one company desperately wants your invention and you have to tell one of them they can't have it? It can get very ugly, and it is not unheard of that you will be sued for all sorts of things if you get yourself into a mess like this. Second, a more focused 'one at a time approach' forces you to look much more closely at the prospects and really do some solid thinking about where your invention would best reside; as well as forcing you to be very attentive to each potential deal and invest the time grooming and cultivating it which may be the difference between success and failure.

You may find that a different approach works better for you, but the 'one at a time' method has always been my preferred approach and the one that has worked best for me.

The license agreement

You've done it! You've found a company that loves your invention and wants to license it from you. Now what? You need to negotiate the terms of a license agreement. There are a few different pieces to license agreements, but the major ones are—the royalty rate, the basis (the number against which royalties are calculated), the royalty advance, and the responsibilities and obligations of both parties, including termination rights.

The royalty rate is probably going to be the most hotly contested aspect of the agreement. You want this to be a big number; the licensee wants it to be a small number. A compromise will likely reside somewhere in the middle—usually between 2% and 7% of net sales. The thing to bear in mind here is that even if you are a great negotiator and you can really beat them up over the rate, it may not be in your best interest to have a very high royalty rate—the reason being that a product burdened by an unusually high royalty load will not only be sold at a higher price point, which may cut down on total sales, but more importantly opens wide the window of opportunity for other companies to swoop in and try to take a piece of the business. You might make more money by accepting a lower royalty rate thereby permitting the product to be sold at a competitive price point which will dramatically expand total sales and also help to ward off the vultures.

The *basis* is actually a much more important figure than the royalty rate—because this is what really determines how much money you will make. The first absolutely inviolable rule is to never, ever sign a deal where you get paid based on a company's 'profits.' As you are probably aware, there is no strict accounting definition of what 'profit' is, and there are as many ways of defining 'profit' as there are people to render an opinion. Unfortunately, with 'profit' being such a plastic concept, it is quite possible to define it in such a way that a company never makes any *profit* when it is convenient for this to be the case. This would mean that if you were getting compensated based on a company's profits you would be waiting a long, long time before you ever saw a check. The proper way to structure a royalty deal is using a basis of 'net sales.' Net sales are basically the total revenues for a given product 'net of' (or minus) certain pre-agreed upon costs. It is these 'costs' that need to be carefully negotiated to come up with a 'net' figure which is fair to both parties, and carries with it the reasonable expectation that you will actually get paid. Again, like 'profit' 'net sales' is a very flexible concept and it can redound to the advantage of one party or the other depending on how it is defined. It is important to arrive at a mutually agreeable definition which allows for legitimate 'costs of sales' but does not too heavily burden the figure with costs which in fairness should be considered 'overhead' or 'costs of doing business.' Some of the permissible deductions (to be subtracted from 'gross' or total sales to arrive at a 'net' figure) are: actual figures or allowances for defects, returns, discounts, and co-op advertising (the shared costs of advertising between the manufacturer and the retailer, but only those directly related to your product). Sometimes companies will try to include deductions for overhead, insurance, yacht maintenance, and all sorts of things which should more appropriately come out of *their* net profits, not yours.

The royalty *advance* is an important concept. It is not intended solely as your 'pay day'—it serves a much more important purpose in the structure of the deal. First, to be clear what we are talking about—a royalty 'advance' is a payment you receive when you execute the license agreement which is basically a 'loan' against future royalties. You are getting some money 'up front' as a token of good faith on the part of the licensee, but generally speaking, they will get to credit this money against 'earned royalties' as sales begin—this means that you will not get another royalty check until the sales have justified a royalty payment in excess of the 'unearned advance' you have already received. Once the advance has been 'recouped' by the company, you will begin to receive regular royalty checks. But again, the point of the advance is not just so you can get some money up front—it serves as an insurance policy that the company you have just licensed your invention to is going to make their best effort to commercialize it. If they have given you a big chunk of change, they will have a strong incentive to try very hard to sell a lot of widgets and earn that money back. If it cost them nothing to tie up your invention, it doesn't really matter to them if they ever get it to market or not—they have nothing to lose.

Some companies will use the argument that they shouldn't have to give you an advance because their 'good faith' should be demonstrated by the substantial investment they will be making in the engineering, tooling, manufacturing, and marketing of your product—and this is a valid point. You, being the clever bastard you are, would counter this by saying, "yes, of course these steps all require substantial investment, and I'm quite sure you'll do everything in your power to recoup your money—but the reason I want an advance is because I want to make sure you actually get to those steps—I want you to have a reason to need to get this product out into the marketplace as quickly as possible."

You've just made a good point, but a savvy company may respond with something along the lines of, "okay, we see your point—you want to make sure that your product is going to see the light of day, and you want to make sure that we have a significant investment in your product so we have a powerful incentive to make a success of it, right?" You nod your head and a big toothy grin spreads across your face because you think you're about to get your big advance. But they go on, "so what we're willing to do is put language in the contract that states that we are obligated to spend 'X' dollars within a certain period of time on the engineering, tooling, manufacturing, and marketing of your invention. Or guarantee that your invention will be commercialized by a certain date. That should address all of your concerns, right?"

At this point, your best bet is probably just to have a temper tantrum, and start beating your fists on the conference table and screaming for your mommy until they give you what you want. Their logic is solid—they have given you everything you claimed to have wanted. So it might be better to start out by saying something along the lines of, "it's true that my desire to have you motivated to make a success of my product has been addressed, but I'd also like to be partially reimbursed up front for the nontrivial development expenses I've incurred, and just to have a token of good faith from you guys that we are entering into a relationship that is going to be lucrative for both of us." Failing that, I have found that flipping over the conference table and taking your invention and going home can be worth a shot.

If you are really lucky, you may not be negotiating a royalty advance, but a license fee. It's like an advance in that it's still a big check you get upon signing the license agreement, but it is not an advance against future royalties—simply a 'bonus' for doing the deal. In this case, you do not have to 'earn' advanced royalties before receiving a royalty check; your royalties will be calculated from the sale of the first product.

If both parties recover from your tantrum, the last piece to be negotiated is the rights and responsibilities of both parties. You will be asked to assert that you are the true owner/inventor of the concept and you have the sole right to enter into the agreement. Be careful with any language relating to a 'hold harmless' or something similar where the company asks you to accept all responsibility for lawsuits or expenses if it turns out that your invention infringes someone else's rights. You can't possibly know this—and you are not representing that you are an intellectual property lawyer or you have any guarantees to offer—all you can say is that you have done your due diligence and, to the best of your knowledge, your invention is unique and proprietary and doesn't infringe. The rest is up to them to figure out. If you accept responsibility for infringing, or grant them a 'hold harmless,' you may find yourself getting the bill for the multi-million dollar legal bill to defend against one or more infringement lawsuits.

One of the important pieces of the agreement is the 'performance' clause which explicitly defines what each party is to do and when. This is where you get commitments about when your product will be first commercialized, etc. Don't dismiss these requirements as being less important than the rest of the agreement—you may find that the success of your invention depends on how thoroughly and unambiguously you spelled out the obligations of each party in the license agreement.

A related clause is the 'minimum guarantee'—this is a set dollar amount which is the minimum the company can pay you each year in royalties or risk termination of the license agreement. The idea behind a minimum is that it again motivates the company to not only commercialize your invention, but to do so aggressively. If they fail to pay you the minimum each year, they have two options—they can give you back the rights to your invention, or they can write a check to bring your annual payments up to the guaranteed level.

You also want to make sure that there is language about what the financial obligations of each party are. Don't sign anything that obliges you to pay for the prosecution or defense of your patent rights; and make sure you see language about the royalty advance or any unearned 'minimum payments' being 'non-recoupable'—meaning you don't have to pay it back if for some reason the company doesn't meet threshold sales volume requirements, or feel that it has been 'earned.'

Finally, you need to make sure that there is some kind of 'exit clause' in the contract—a way for you to disentangle yourself from this company and get back the rights to your invention if they fail to perform or if the relationship just doesn't work out.

Exclusivity

One of the key aspects of licensing is 'exclusivity' or the granting of rights in your invention to only one entity. This is almost always the best way to proceed. The minute you start trying to chop up the rights to your invention so you can license it to more than one party, you will get into trouble. First of all, if a company knows it isn't getting exclusive rights, the value of your invention to them is greatly reduced. Second, you will create endless problems with semantics and definitions about how you divide up territories or market segments so companies are not stepping on one another's toes constantly. A non-exclusive license may seem like a good idea and a way to maximize the financial returns from your invention, but in my experience it leads to a great deal more trouble and overall diminished value as compared to an exclusive arrangement with a carefully selected licensing partner.

Putting It All Together

Congratulations—you've made it to the end of the road—we have covered all of the relevant pieces of what makes an invention a commercially viable product—and how you can make it happen and make money from it. As a final exercise, let's take a look at a case history—follow an invention from the beginning of the process right through to the profits from commercialization.

For illustration purposes, I'm going to use an invention of mine which has not yet found a home because it would be unfair to my clients (and potentially incriminating to me) to divulge the behind the scenes details of products that are actually out in the world being sold by companies whose names you know. The process is identical; the only difference is that the story ends with a question mark, not a royalty check.

The opportunity

Even though you might not guess it from my physique, I like to work out regularly with free weights. It is common knowledge that in order for a muscle to grow stronger, you must exercise it to the point of failure. With most exercises, reaching the point of failure means that you can no longer pick up the weights, or you can't complete a rep, or the weights go crashing to the floor. With a bench press exercise, however, reaching the point of failure presents a much more interesting complication—basically, you end up trapped under the barbell—because with a bench press, the only safe way to finish the exercise is by completing a rep. If, by definition, muscle failure means the inability to complete a rep—you're in for trouble.

This seemed the perfect opportunity for a clever solution—an invention—because the very real and practical need I was experiencing had to be a problem faced by many, and there is a robust exercise equipment market filled with manufacturers/marketers always on the lookout for the latest gadget.

Notice that I haven't pointed out the safety benefits of my system—there is a reason for this. Safety doesn't sell. It seems crazy, but people will spend money for things that look good, feel good, smell good, do something, do nothing—in short they'll spend money on pretty much anything and everything, but if you try to get them to ante up a little bit extra for a safety feature, you might as well be whistling Dixie. I don't condone this, I don't pretend to understand it—I point it out simply as a warning for those altruistic souls out there bent on saving the world. You'd do better refining your hover toilet idea, I assure you.

Problem solving

Back to the matter at hand-- there are two potential solutions to the problem of muscle failure and the incomplete rep on the bench press—either you stop short of the point of failure so you are never at risk of not being able to finish a rep and ending up trapped under the barbell; or you have a spotter. There are problems with both options—if you stop exercising before you reach muscle failure, you will not get stronger—you will soon reach a plateau in your workouts and progress will grind to a halt. If you opt for the 'spotter' route, you have to first find a spotter who is available when you want to work out, and then you have the problem of communicating with them. Bear in mind that the moment when you need a spot is the precise moment when you are least able to articulate what you need. To put it another way, if you are straining with your last reserves of strength to get a big, heavy piece of iron off of your chest, this is probably not the time you'd like to have a nice chat about the weather. Obviously, you're not going to be talking with your spotter about such trivialities, but the point is you will be hard pressed to utter much more than a grunt at a time when the concise, accurate articulation of just how much assistance you require at precisely which points in the range of motion are what is really required in order for the spot to be of value. The curious thing about a spot is that even though you may be lifting hundreds of pounds, it is frequently only a matter of ounces or a few pounds which need to be 'relieved' by the spotter in order for you to complete the rep, and generally speaking this 'help' is needed only at a specific and narrowly defined point in the overall range of motion of the exercise. If you are not able to communicate this to the spotter, it is very likely that they will 'help' too much, thereby pretty much negating the benefit of the 'forced rep' and cheating you out of the muscle failure you'd been striving for.

I don't particularly care for the social, hygienic, or competitive aspects of membership gyms, so I work out in my home. I have a nicely equipped gym and I can get a good workout. The problem is that I don't have a spotter available, so my only real option for my bench press workouts, made painfully clear the first few times I tried rolling, then tipping a fully loaded barbell off my chest when I couldn't lift it up to the bench's vertical support stanchions, was to stop my bench press workouts short of complete muscle failure. As predicted, I soon reached a plateau in my bench press weights which I couldn't break through.

I did a little research and found that nobody made any kind of self-spotting bench. There were a few products out there that called themselves 'self spotting' but they weren't what I was looking for—they were either 'safety stops' (simply lower travel limits which would prevent the bar from crushing you), or 'powered lifters' (devices which employed some sort of powered lifting system to raise the bar off of you when you can no longer lift it. None of these was what I was looking for—I wanted all of the features and benefits of a human spotter without having to have a big hairy guy standing over me dripping sweat.

Proof of concept

Short of dragging my housekeeper into the gym, it occurred to me that there had to be a mechanical solution to this problem. I figured that while I'm doing a bench press exercise I'm lying down employing very few of my muscles; and all I really need is a very small amount of assistance for a spot—there's gotta be a way of spotting myself. But how? The answer came in two parts—it dawned on me that not only are my legs pretty much not involved in the bench press motion, they are far and away the strongest muscles in my body. If I could somehow employ their strength during a bench press, I could easily spot myself. But my legs, it happened, were rather far away from the barbell—too far to be of much use. Here is where the second part of the solution came in—I reasoned that there had to be a relatively simple mechanical means of transferring the power and motion of my legs to the barbell.

There were a number of requirements to be met—the involvement of my legs could not compromise the safety or efficacy of the basic exercise, the movement and muscle/joint loading had to be biomechanically safe, the 'assist' or spot had to be proportional and fully controllable, the mechanical means could not be bulky, complex, expensive, or in any way limit or interfere with the utility of the bench, and the mechanical means could not alter or undermine the principal benefit of free weights—the unencumbered three axis freedom of motion which theoretically engages many more muscles and develops coordination and fine motor skills, unlike stack loaded machines with a narrowly defined and controlled path of motion.

As I studied the problem, it occurred to me that many consumer weight benches come with a leg extension adaptor which 'doubles' the utility of the bench. It can be used both for bench work as well as for leg extensions. This got me thinking—if I were to attach a leg extension device to the bench, would I be able to operate it while laying flat on my back and doing a bench press? Easy to figure out—I tried, and I could. Great—now I had a means of harnessing the mechanical energy of my legs. I then called a sports medicine doctor friend of mine and he assured me that using my legs in this way would be safe during the bench press exercise. All that remained was to figure out how to get this force to the proper location and vector (direction and magnitude).

I sketched out a cable and a series of pulleys, which would be routed from the leg extension device, under the bench, then along an upright into a 'gallows' style overhead unit which ultimately would attach to the center of the barbell. I found I needed to 'stretch' the bench—increase the length so my knees would line up with the leg extension device when my chest was properly located under the barbell, and add a cable tensioner to allow enough 'slack' in the cable for a normal range of motion of the barbell without engaging the cable or allowing it to fall out of the pulleys. And with a basic sketch in hand, I fabricated a few pieces and 'bread boarded' the concept. Actually, it turned out to be more of a *prototype* because I used the same style square tubing, end caps, pulleys and cable, and white powder-coating that are used in most exercise equipment, so the add-on parts ended up looking like they had been designed and built onto the bench at the factory. It's funny how closely the initial sketch resembles the final design, but it has a simple elegance to it. The only details I left out of the prototype were the features which would make the unit adjustable to accommodate different size users. I had figured out how to do this, I just didn't bother with it because I'm the only one who uses this particular bench. Also, the means of attaching the cable to the barbell is something I designed, but implemented in a different way for the prototype.

The thing that really surprised me was how incredibly effective the invention was—I had intended it as pretty much a 'safety net' which would allow me to push my last rep or two and not have to worry about getting trapped under the bar; but it turned out to be something entirely different—it revolutionized my workouts.

I had never realized the full extent of the subconscious 'trauma' I had experienced when I was 'trapped' under the barbell. It really was quite unpleasant having to roll a heavy bar down my chest and abdomen before being able to get out from under it—but I didn't know quite how acutely my subconscious wanted to avoid a repetition of the event.

This only became clear to me once I tried my first workout on the newly modified bench. I tried the leg extension/pulley system right away to make sure it worked, was strong enough, and felt right. It checked out okay, so I began to go through my regular 'pyramid sets' (a workout routine where you gradually increase the weight and decrease the number of reps). Surprisingly, I zipped right past my previous 'max' weight, and kept right on going! I thought this must be a fluke—some extra energy stemming from the exuberance of having a nifty new invention to play with or something—but it kept happening. Over and over again, during each successive workout, I would set new 'high limits' and have really great results—*without ever having to use the self-spotting feature.* Only after I'd been enjoying the benefits for a while did it occur to me that the 'self spotting' aspect wasn't just a safety feature—it totally removed the psychological limits and bar-riers I had been subconsciously dealing with which were really hindering my workouts. When I finally did have an opportunity to use the self-spotting feature, it became instantly apparent that not only was this 'as good as' a human spotter—it was much better. Again, the issue of communication is a big problem with a traditional spotter but with my unit I no longer had a flawed 'open' system which relied on verbal communication under difficult conditions, but instead had a 'closed loop system'—I knew ex-actly when and how much of a spot I needed, and I could give that to myself without having to utter a word. And the action of using my legs to spot didn't interfere in any way with my bench work. It could not have been a better result. I showed the 'self spot-ting bench' to a few friends who were also into free weight workouts and they all agreed—an amazing benefit.

Here was an example of an 'accidental invention' of sorts—not like Post It Notes which were a total fluke, but my invention solved problems and provided benefits I didn't even realize existed prior to undertaking the project.

Before attempting to find a licensee, I filed a provisional patent application. This involved a search of the prior art, or novelty search to determine what related inventions were already patented, how broad the protection I was likely to be able to secure might be, and whether I was infringing anybody else's patents. I found the category to be only lightly traveled and determined that I would be likely to secure broad protection for an invention that could be commercialized without infringing any other patents. I also made every effort to include every conceivable embodiment or fundamentally different solution to the same problem in my patent application to insure that I had as broad an 'estate of intellectual property' or buffer zone around my core invention as possible.

Refinement

So now it dawned on me that a project which had started out as a solution to a personal need had all of the hallmarks of a legitimate 'invention' with commercial potential. I revisited the design and came up with a few more tweaks that I thought would make the unit less costly to produce and improve the functionality and flexibility (size adjustability). I also changed the geometry slightly so the unit could 'spot' overhead press work as well. And I documented the design with some drawings, photographs, a written description, and a short video.

Monetization

With my rights and date of invention protected, I began researching exercise equipment manufacturers. Since in my mind this was still sort of a 'pet' project—just something I was doing for my own benefit, but which might have commercial potential, I used a somewhat different criterion for identifying a suitable target company to approach-- I looked for a company that was geographically convenient. Of course, I wanted a company that seemed to be an innovator and had a recognized, respected brand name, and I found a couple not far from Los Angeles where I live.

I made a few phone calls, and was able to not only speak to the founder/owner of one of these companies, but I was able to get him to sign my standard Confidential Disclosure Agreement. So far, so good. We set up a meeting at his factory for the following week and I headed out there with high hopes. When I arrived at his rather sprawling facility, I was somewhat taken aback by a general feeling of 'emptiness' of the place—it was a large factory spanning several buildings, but there seemed to be very few workers, very little product, and lots of empty space. The owner explained that this was because most of their production was shifting offshore; but it did not inspire confidence or give the impression of a company doing booming business.

When we finally sat down in the conference room and I pitched my idea, I was pleasantly surprised by the reaction I got—it seemed that these guys really 'got' the idea and found it to be both novel and useful. They thought they could market a product like this. Cool.

Then the owner asked with some concern what I hoped to get out of this. Reasoning that I had very little invested in the project, and sensing that money was something of an issue for these guys, I gave him an answer that pleased him no end, but probably created a problem for me. I said, "I'm not looking to make money at somebody else's expense—I am only interested in making money when my partners are making money. Don't give me anything up front—I'll help you get the unit into production, then you just pay me a royalty on each unit sold. That way you never have to reach into your pocket to pay me—I make money when you make money." They loved it, and we hammered out a simple license agreement on the spot.

We also talked about what the development cycle was going to look like. They were going to build a new prototype in their in-house fabrication shop, and they were going to do it aggressively because there were dates which were rapidly approaching for catalog deadlines as well as a number of major fitness equipment shows they attended at which they wanted to be able to exhibit their 'new product.'

So I left feeling as though I had just made a nice deal. Not a homerun by any means, but maybe I'd make a few bucks off of something that had originated as a personal project. The problem was that it became both increasingly difficult to reach my new business partner by phone over the next few months, as well as increasingly apparent that they weren't doing anything at all with my invention. I realized that my first impression when touring their facility that this was a company in trouble was probably accurate. After giving it a bit more time, I finally sent them a certified letter stating that based on their failure to perform, I was withdrawing my invention from them and terminating our license agreement. I received a terse acknowledgement, and that was the end of this relationship.

As I look back on this failed deal, I realize that my biggest mistake was in attempting to be gracious and accommodating by not insisting on some kind of royalty advance. The point of an advance is not just to make a few bucks up front—it's to make sure the licensee has something to lose if they don't perform—an incentive to make a commercial success of the invention they have licensed from you.

I soon found another fitness equipment manufacturer who was interested in the self-spotting bench; but because I wasn't convinced that I wanted to enter into another license agreement—thinking that I might want to manufacture and market the invention myself, I simply asked this new company to build a production reflective prototype and once we had clarified production costs, appearance, and functionality, we could discuss whether they wanted to add the product to their line or just act as a contract manufacturer for me.

I had begun to believe that this might be a good product to 'manufacture' and market myself because I could find a contract manufacturer to deliver packaged, turn-key product, and I could leverage personal relationships to find a celebrity endorser and a prominent fitness web marketer to help create consumer awareness and demand.

Remarkably, I found myself in a similar situation to the first—week after week I would call the owner of the small fitness equipment manufacturing company and he would explain how they had been extremely busy this week but they would definitely get the prototype built next week. And the next week. And the next week. The difference in this case was that they were legitimately busy and simply overwhelmed with orders rather than in a death spiral, but the end result was the same—no prototype.

So I found myself back at square one with my 'self-spotting bench.' I am currently in discussions with yet another fitness equipment manufacturer/marketer, also potentially interested in adding my invention to their product line; but I am beginning to consider an entirely different avenue to commercialization—I had originally thought to manufacture the product locally and domestically as a high end 'pro-sumer' grade product; but I am now considering developing a low cost, high volume manufacturing source in China and re-positioning the product as a mass market item.

I'm not entirely certain which direction the project will take, but I am confident that one way or another we will get the self-spotting bench into the marketplace. Stay tuned...

A few things to watch out for.

This should probably be entitled, "A few MORE things to watch out for," as there are no end of pitfalls and pratfalls to be wary of; but there are a few other potential problems I wanted to make you aware of which didn't seem to fit organically into any of the other discussions.

First, I can't emphasize enough how important it is to maintain a sense of objectivity about your invention throughout the development process. While this may seem somewhat at odds with my earlier advice to hang in there and persevere regardless of adversity, opposition, or repeated rejection, there is a point beyond which continued effort is no longer perseverance, it's insanity. While I don't recommend paying much heed to others' opinions and advice, if every person you encounter, particularly those with some grounding in invention or development, or just your really smart friends tell you without exception that they don't 'get it,' well, it may be time to move on. No idea is worth losing friends, family, or quality of life over.

Which brings up the second point—don't allow an idea to become 'precious.' What do I mean by this?

Simply that you must maintain both perspective and an open mind about your idea and the possibility that it may not be the best, only, or greatest way to solve a problem, let alone the most magnificent idea of all time. As we earlier alluded to, allowing your idea to become precious can not only blind you to alternative or possibly better solutions to the same problem, it can open an enormous window of opportunity through which your competition can jump. I've dealt many times with inventors who were so in love with their ideas that they couldn't imagine there was a better way to skin that particular cat—in many cases investing tens or hundreds of thousands of dollars in development, patents, business startups—only to be shocked and embarrassed when I casually pointed out a better, cheaper, and completely unrelated (non-infringing) way to do the same thing. Ooops. The best advice I can offer in this regard is to do what I do when I'm coming up with an invention or trying to solve a problem—work your genius idea to the point where you're absolutely confident you have something great, then put it aside and start from scratch—a clean sheet of paper, with the only rule being that you can't use the previous idea as a starting point or work on something in any way related. Oftentimes you'll find that your first idea was a good one, but your new ideas may afford you a different understanding of issues or solutions.

Finally, and this one might be better submitted to a Psychology journal—be realistic about the possibility that your invention may not ultimately come to fruition, and don't let a fear of this cause you to drag the development out forever in an effort to delay the inevitable moment of truth wherein the market accepts or rejects your invention.

What am I talking about? I would have thought that this was an absolutely ridiculous concept until I began noticing a pattern with a few of my consulting clients—they would talk incessantly about how they couldn't wait to get their new product to market and make lots of money and be enormously successful;

but somehow every time we would get close to that point where we would actually find out if the market was interested in the product, my client would suddenly find a need for a fundamental redesign, or become obsessed with some new detail we simply had to include in the product, necessitating yet another redesign or tooling change. I've had a number of these clients where this process was drawn out over more than a few years. Eventually, it became clear to me that even though they truly did want the product to be successful, and they really wanted to make money from it, the risk that the product might not be successful was so overwhelmingly terrifying that they couldn't take a chance of ever getting to the point of finding out—even if that meant they'd by definition also never know if the product would have been successful. In other words—their perceived risk of failure was greater than their desire for success.

As you can well imagine, that's neither a healthy nor a productive attitude to have. I suppose that the underlying motivation is much the same thing that drives many of us to want to invent in the first place—we do it because we want to feel that we're working towards the possibility of some great success; we want to feel as though there's at least a chance that we will succeed and accomplish our dreams. But if this drive becomes twisted into a need to have something perpetually in development, and an avoidance at all costs of ever being tested—you are no longer an inventor, you are a poser. Invention is full of risk, full of failure—but equally, it is filled with opportunity and success. Try. Keep trying. Fail. Keep failing. Then try some more—and eventually you will succeed. And the sweetness of that success more than offsets everything that preceded it.

That's all folks...

So there you have it—a quick course on the business of inventing. Hopefully I've covered all of the major points and given you enough information and sufficient guidance that you can confidently undertake to develop an invention of your own. Don't for a minute think that there isn't a great deal more to learn and understand—in fact one of the things I love most about being an 'inventor' is that there is no 'end game'—you can never wake up one day and say, "I've done it all—I know everything there is to know about being an inventor."

Every day presents new challenges and opportunities, and you now have the tools to make of them what you will. Remember—the difference between doing *something* and doing *nothing* is getting up off your ass and making it happen. No more excuses— you can now be an 'inventor,' or 'a person sitting on the couch who once read a book about inventing.' It's your choice.

www.ingramcontent.com/pod-product-compliance
Lightning Source LLC
Chambersburg PA
CBHW051446170526
45166CB00001B/135